# VINTAGE LORRY ANNUAL

EDITED by NICK BALDWIN

PUBLISHED BY
MARSHALL HARRIS & BALDWIN LTD
17 AIR STREET LONDON W1

# INTRODUCING OURSELVES

THIS Vintage Annual is the first of many from an important new name in transport publishing. Though Marshall, Harris & Baldwin Ltd may be new, its background most certainly is not. Prince Marshall and Brian Harris were the original founders of *OLD MOTOR MAGAZINE*, which they successfully ran for over sixteen years and which was the first publication to give equal coverage to pre-1960 cars, commercials, bikes and steam vehicles. They were later joined by Nick Baldwin, the editor of this Annual, who had previously worked on such magazines as *Autocar*, *Motor Transport* and *Automobile Engineer*, and whose motor publishing experience, when added to that of Prince and Brian's, amounts to some seventy years of editorial, production and design.

During the period they have built up an unrivalled archive of transport photographs and information which they plan to put to good use in the future in a series of Kaleidoscope Books on different aspects of transport history. So far, Kaleido-scopes on Farm Tractors, Motorcycles and Lorries have been produced and more specialist titles are on the way, such as Richard Shuttleworth, Leo Villa's life with the Campbells, Shelvoke and Drewry commercial vehicles, Steam Wagons, AC Cars, and many more. In addition, we shall be producing regular Vintage Annuals on a variety of subjects - including this one on Trucks, one on Cars of all ages, one on Buses, another on Motorcycling, and, hopefully, before long, one on Farm Tractors and Machinery as well.

Most publishers would steer clear of these subjects in their pursuit of such lucrative markets as 'classic' cars and traction engines, but we feel that minority subjects are just as important to the study of transport and that after twenty years of preserving and writing about offbeat and popular vehicles, we know what an important section of the old vehicle movement wants. We hope you agree, and that you enjoy this unique medley of articles and photographs and that you will buy future editions of the Vintage Lorry Annual each year.

The study of trucks and trucking is now both an absorbing hobby for the enthusiast and a pleasant pastime for the thousands involved in the industry who take an active interest in the past. In our own small way we have contributed to this movement, which was virtually unknown when we launched the magazine *VINTAGE COMMERCIAL* in 1962 (which later merged with *OLD MOTOR*) and we were closely involved with the pioneer days of truck and bus preservation even before that. We have watched the growth of the Historic Commercial Vehicle Club and the interest in truck history with great satisfaction and feel that our Vintage Annuals and Kaleidoscopes are the best way in which we can share our love of the subject with transport friends old and new.

Let us know what you think of the results and also of your latest vehicle and archive discoveries and restorations. We cannot promise to reply to all our correspondents, but what you tell us will be of immense value in planning future issues, as well as for building up a useful 'letters and news' section in our 1980 edition.

# BATH TUBS TO BEER BOTTLES, THE STORY OF
# ADVERTISING VEHICLES

**There has been a long tradition of using delivery vehicles for publicity purposes.
In the early days an eye-catching special body was financially feasible
whilst today it is the memorable livery that is all-important.
ARTHUR INGRAM has been looking at some of the more bizarre examples
of advertising vehicles over the years.**

IT was not long after the introduction of the motor vehicle that advertisers realised the potential of a mobile and self contained unit which could carry out the dual rôles of billboard and delivery vehicle.

Many brand names began to appear on the lighter vans and trucks of the period, and there was much activity among bodybuilders to provide something which was both striking and original. Some enterprising publicity firms in the early twenties even hired the space on the side of big general delivery vans and

then offered it as a mobile hoarding to national advertisers.

With much less vehicle legislation to contain his exuberance, the adventurous bodybuilder of the teens and twenties was able to unleash upon the buying public a wide variety of designs guaranteed to turn the head of any unsuspecting consumer.

There were many famous names all vying with one another for a share of their particular market and for little extra cost when compared with an ordinary van (which, after

all, was equally hand built in those days) they could have something as unusual as a biscuit tin or ink bottle shaped body on conventional chassis/cabs. Others strove hard to provide a bottle of beer on wheels or a mobile bathtub complete with geyser!

Tea, tyres, boot polish, biscuits, sweets and cigarettes were all regularly advertised by way of specially shaped bodies behind the

**A natty little Morris Minor pretending to be a lamp bulb package.**

A cleverly disguised fleet of Morris car chassis in the twenties publicising vacuum cleaners.

More short term publicity in the form of an unidentified American vehicle dressed up for a gala in Capetown.

cab. More interesting, although rarer, were those vehicles which appeared as the advertised article entirely covering the vehicle with only the minimum of necessary windscreen and radiator showing. The Watney's beer barrel came into this category as did the Kolynos toothpaste tube, Electrolux vacuum cleaner, Ewarts hot water geyser, Bass and Worthington beer bottles of a few years back, while in more recent times we have seen the Sugar Puffs train, the Mann Crossman Main Line locomotive and the Euro-exhaust silencer and exhaust pipes.

Unfortunately, in recent years there has been a decline in the number of advertising vehicles used in the streets. Reasons for this are not difficult to establish, what with prohibitive labour costs and lack of custom body experience and an almost unending string of vehicle legislation which seriously hampers the advertising vehicle designers and bodybuilders. Licensing costs are also a great deterrent because many of the designs leave little or no room for the carriage of goods, save for perhaps a few parcels of literature or samples. In recent years the advertising budgets of large companies have been drastically reduced as vehicle building and operating costs have soared. Many a marketing director must have decided that with the need to keep his products right up to date it may be necessary to revise the company image or house style at frequent intervals. Hence a vehicle built as a 1979 package may be decidedly obsolete by 1981, and whereas a plain box van can be re-written or the stick-on variety of lettering replaced quite quickly and cheaply, a new advertising vehicle is just not on.

A useful vehicle for soliciting magazine subscriptions when it toured agricultural markets. The chassis is an Austin 12.

So as we savour some of the unique designs of days long past we can muse on which vehicle made the most impact - or is that the right word? Evidently the police thought just that when they saw the advertising ploy of one operator about 50 years ago, for he had built a bonnet, cab and tilt van body on a period proprietory chassis. Nothing unusual about that, you say - no, until you find he mounted the whole thing back-to-front so that the driver sat hidden inside the tilt body and the vehicle was driven along the road 'backwards'!

Another facet of advertising vehicles has been to use ordinary vehicles in unusual guises. Instances of this include the American ready mixed concrete firm which converted a BMC Mini into a six wheeler and mounted a scaled down version of a truck mixer drum on the back. Another Mini was converted to a tractor unit by a Canadian operator who then built a scale tandem axle van trailer based on his full size long distance trucks.

Largest of these miniature vehicles - if you know what we mean, is undoubtedly the half size Peterbilt cabover double bottom outfit built and operated by the American PIE concern. Although produced at considerable cost, the operators consider it a wise advertising investment and it has been widely used at truck rodeos and safety conventions across the country. In Britain, such firms as Stevens and Albany build 'replica' vintage vans to offer something out of the ordinary to publicity conscious operators, but the days of mobile loaves and ink pots are gone forever - or are they? Perhaps not, in the growing tide of individualism.

Driving this Austin 7 bath tub was not a job for the shy - though clothes were worn!

A simpler and perhaps more practical publicity vehicle on an unmodified Graham/Dodge truck. Presumably only samples were carried.

Presumably also for a one-off pageant, as the driver's vision would be rather too impaired for general use!

There was a craze for streamlining in the thirties and this converted car would have been extremely eye-catching.

A Ford 8 spotted by Arthur Ingram at Kings Cross in 1952 publicising a long forgotten brand of lager.

A 1925 Fiat 502F 15 cwt chassis dressed up as a radio valve for Mullard.

A 1952 10 cwt Ford makes an eye-catching portable beer barrel with a certain amount of load space when the rear of the barrel is hinged open.

Perhaps the most famous 'beer bottle' was the Worthington Daimler with its neck lying along the bonnet top and its crown cork blending with the frilly Daimler radiator. This is Bass' answer to it in 1957 on a Seddon chassis.

Brewers seem to have had more money to indulge their publicity whims and here is another example from the fifties.

A 1952 Austin three-way van built primarily for publicity purposes.

Pacific Intermountain Express' famous half scale Peterbilt cabover. Several other examples have been made in the States, including a bonneted Kenworth of similar size.

The Mini has come in for some interesting commercial customising. This trick photo shows a genuine Mini artic outfit made in Canada to publicise pies, with a scaled down man beside it.

A new way to look distinctive is to buy a modern van with ancient styling. This is one of the most realistic and is made by Albany at Christchurch. The original prototype belonging to their Sales Representative, Lawrence Sheffer, is shown.

GEORGE PERRY goes to visit

# A MAN WITH A MAUDSLAY IN HIS GARDEN

THERE'S a word for collectors of stamps, postcards, butterflies - and even matchboxes, but no one has so far coined one for people who collect lorries. Possibly because as yet such collectors are few, since it is a hobby that demands, among other things, a considerable amount of space.

Peter Davies, a lorry enthusiast for as long as he can remember, got the yen to have his very own rigid eight-wheeler in the sixties. At the time he was living in an ordinary semi-detached house. 'Buying a lorry without the space to keep it is a crazy move,' he says. 'I'd never make a general, would I?' Luckily, there was a farmer or two in the Hertfordshire

Peter Davies' Meritor, soon after it had been sold by Maudslay to a crane hire firm, from whom he bought it in 1966.

A man-sized radiator gets a top-up, not in a transport yard but in a Flitwick back garden.

and Bedfordshire area who, spotting his advertisement in the local press, was able to offer a barn in return for a modest rental. That is, until Peter Davies was able to move to larger premises, necessary also for his collection of 20,000 photographs, books, bound volumes of *Commercial Motor*, catalogues, drawings and other material pertaining to lorries.

He lives now in a modern, detached house at Flitwick, a few minutes' drive north of Luton, where he works as an advertising specialist for Vauxhall. Or, more specifically, the Bedford truck division, where his responsibilities include preparing technical sales force information, producing literature and organising shows. He first joined Vauxhall more than twenty years ago as a commercial apprentice, after wanting to be a diesel engineer. Somehow he gravitated into an artistic area, but has always in his career been close to his passion - commercial vehicles. 'When I started, the biggest thing Bedford built was their seven tonner. Now look at them. On the other hand, my department has shrunk in size - now there's just six of us. That's because Vauxhall have split the cars from the commercials. But because I work there, people think I'm a Bedford enthusiast. My interests go way beyond that'.

What really entrance him are the vehicles that pounded along Britain's roads when he was a boy. He was born in 1940. His dream would be for haulage operators still to run them today, but realising that such a romantic fancy would be somewhat impractical, he regards as the next best thing for preservationists like himself to keep a representative sample in working order.

'When I started, hardly anyone was preserving heavy lorries,' he says. 'The first one I went after was a Chinese Six Albion I'd heard about running in North London, but I was too late - it had gone for scrap. Then I went up to Liverpool to see a Maudslay Eight, and another in Scotland. Neither was any good. Then coming down the motorway I saw a Maudslay Eight coming towards me. It was an amazing sight - they'd nearly all been scrapped by then. There was no way to identify it, all it had on the side was the

Peter Davies surveys the Meritor - so typical of the 'no frills' attitude of its day.

The Maudslay had a narrow escape in 1969 when the land on which it stood caught fire. Luckily the damage was not too serious, thanks to the speedy intervention of the Vauxhall fire brigade.

Maudslay shield. So I wrote to *Commercial Motor*. Eventually I found that it belonged to a Birmingham plant hire firm, who had bought it from Maudslay themselves and were running it. I raced up there to do a deal. That was December 1966'.

They told him that the scrap value was £350, and he in turn offered a paltry £150. So they compromised, and let him have it for £270. It wasn't even registered, being ex-works, and at first it carried an anachronistic number plate with an 'E' suffix letter. But in time he was able to get a more appropriate registration, MUG 340, a Leeds number of 1949, well within the period when such vehicles were built. In fact, the Maudslay Meritor, of which this is an example, was in production from September 1947 until January 1951. Only 256 were built, and Peter Davies' specimen is number 254, completed on 26th January 1951, at the Parkside Works, Coventry.

Having bought his lorry, the next

problem was its restoration. Owning a heavy vehicle is not light on the pocket, even if accommodation is not taken into account. A set of tyres can cost £1000, a set of batteries £120. And relining the brakes could run to £400. Filling the tank to take her on the road at present prices for diesel represents nearly £40 straight out of the wallet. Luckily, the old pals' network came to the rescue, and spares, tyres and so on were found at low prices. Also, although the behemoth is 30ft long with a 17ft 6ins wheelbase, it can be taxed at the same rate as a private car, if it is not used commercially. And insurance can be had through the Historic Commercial Vehicle Club for a mere £15.00.

Peter Davies doesn't care overmuch for rallies. What he really hates is the sight of old vehicles so cosmeticised with paint, varnish and polished brightwork that they look totally unnatural, even if they do win prizes for turnout. He likes a lorry to look like one that is actually working for its living. Had his Maudslay originally belonged to a haulage firm, he would have restored it to its former appearance, but in this case he has had to use his artistic skills to invent a livery appropriate to a

private company on the eve of nationalisation. He has used navy blue with gold lining, and on the cab doors painted a crest, incorporating a monogram made up of his initials. Across the front of the cream painted cab roof is a slogan 'Send it by road'. Various destination points from one end of Britain to the other are inscribed along the sides. There is a flat load of timber under the securely roped tarpaulin. Only a set of more recent trafficators ('It didn't even have semaphores when it was built') belie the absolute authenticity of its appearance.

'I've really wanted it to look right. In fact, I've been out on the road in it, and I've had lorry drivers fail to appreciate that it was a preserved vehicle. "Fancy working for a firm with old tackle like that!" they've said'.

Early in its time in Peter Davies' ownership, the old Maudslay was involved in an unlikely hazard. An oil reservoir half a mile from his former house burst its banks, and flooded the entire neighbourhood with thousands of gallons of black, sticky ooze. The lorry was then on hardstanding in his garden, and soon was up to its wheel rims in oil. When eventually the mess was

The Maudslay poses outside its shed whilst inside Peter Davies' next project, a Sentinel diesel, waits patiently.

cleared and the authorities had arranged for tons of sand to be put down, he was able to take advantage of a successful insurance claim and have the hardstanding renewed. Meanwhile, the oil had permeated the ground. 'We were sitting on a time bomb and didn't know it!' Months later, when the work began, one of the contractor's labourers tried to dispose of an old shed by burning it. To his consternation the entire garden, by now totally oil-ridden, went up in flames. Only the prompt arrival of Vauxhall's fire brigade prevented the Maudslay from being consumed in the holocaust. As it was, it lost its tyres, tarpaulin and suffered a burnt cab roof. 'Unfortunately, I didn't realise it at the time, but the sides of the cab became distorted in the fire, and even now you can see a slight buckling. That was in 1968, since when she has had a cloudless existence. I average about a thousand miles a year in her'.

In 1970 he acquired a second vehicle - a 1948 Sentinel diesel, which was formerly an oxygen carrier for the BOC. Restoration work is taking a long time, but eventually he hopes to have it looking as good as the Maudslay. They sit in a specially built garage, 33ft long and 22ft wide, behind his house at Flitwick. But what will he eventually do with them?

'I want to go on running the Maudslay indefinitely, but I don't think that I can hand them on to my children, as they are both girls. I don't expect my wife to share my enthusiasm - I'd think her a bit weird if she did. I'll probably donate them - I hope by then to a National Commercial Collection. I hate the word museum. I'd like people to see these vehicles running'.

### MAUDSLAY MERITOR
Eight wheel rigid heavy lorry
7 tons 10 cwt laden, 22 tons gross
Wheelbase: 17ft 6ins.
Length: 30ft. Bodywork: 24ft 6ins.
AEC 9.6 litre diesel engine.
Five-speed constant mesh gearbox
Kirkstall axles.
Built: January 1951, Parkside
   Works, Coventry.

Adding to the genuine period look of the vehicle is this realistically sheeted 'load'.

Air conditioning 1951 style! It may have been spartan and slow but it always got there in the end and could still be earning its keep today if modern drivers could put up with the discomfort.

# TRUCKS ON TRACKS

**Best known today for their 4x4 farm tractors, Roadless began by applying
First World War tank track technology to the art of moving heavy loads
across rough country.
As these unique photographs show,
a fascinating variety of vintage trucks came in for their unusual treatment.**

THE First World War showed the army and vehicle engineers how helpless the average vehicle was when it left the metalled road. Tracks enabled large tractors and tanks to work on soft ground with

some success, though the primitive tracks did not conform with rough ground and if too little of them was in contact they soon lost traction and allowed the vehicle to sink.

In the tank design department of

the War Department, Lt Col Philip Johnson gained wide experience of tracks and when peace came amidst confidence that there would never be another war, he decided to put his ideas and discoveries to civilian use.

One of a large fleet of Roadless equipped Morris-Commercials is put through its paces in the mid-twenties before shipment overseas by the Anglo-Persian Oil Co.

The considerable flexibility of the Roadless track and suspension is demonstrated by a Morris turning and climbing out of ruts.

He formed Roadless Traction Ltd in 1919 and was joined by his wartime friend Charles Shelton, who became works manager, and by C W Clark, E L Firth and G J Rackham, who was later to find fame at AEC. An American company holding Roadless patents was also formed to exploit Johnson's ideas and sell them to the motor industry there - indeed they sold production rights to the International Motor Co - the makers

Works drawing of a 1922 Mack 2½ tonner with Roadless equipment built under licence from Roadless Patents Holding Co, Washington.

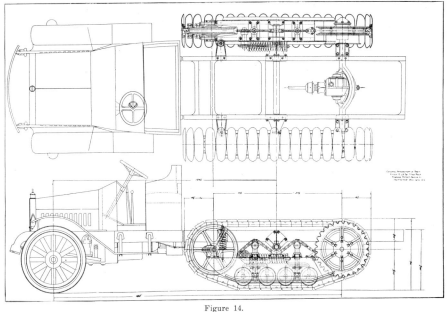

Figure 14.

FWDs were particularly suited to half tracks as the driven front axle stopped the wheels from being forced into the ground by the tracks. These are both ex-WD American trucks rebuilt in Britain in 1924/5.

---

With the aid of half tracks, a demonstration AEC converted by the makers successfully negotiates impossible conditions for a solid tyred three tonner.

---

More Morris-Commercials than any other make were converted by Roadless. They were cheap, simple, strong and flexible. Note the extra deep radiator header tank to cope with constant low gear work and to keep the coolant above the block on extreme gradients.

- the makers of Mack trucks - in the early twenties.

Roadless concentrated on light and flexible tracks (experimenting initially with an Overland car on full tracks) that could yield locally to small objects yet not exert any greater pressure on them than on the ground under the rest of the track. They achieved this by spring loading the distance between the driving sprocket and idler wheels with cables and coil springs. The tracks could either be full, as on a four ton truck with coal scuttle bonnet built by Roadless in 1922, or half, which could be substituted for the back wheels on any make of truck. To begin with the half tracks were very long to give minimum ground pressure. To overcome their reluctance to let the front wheels steer the vehicle, they were given spherical joints between the stamped steel links, and these permitted the tracks to follow the line of the front wheels, even down to a 17 foot radius without side slip on the two ton Vulcan.

A Foden steamer was so equipped in 1922 and it worked well with five tons aboard, though widening rings had to be fitted to the solid front tyres to avoid them ploughing into soft ground. Henceforth, most of the heavy vehicles given Roadless equipment were FWDs, whose driven front axle avoided this problem. Lighter vehicles escaped this difficulty and several firms offered chassis specially designed for Roadless tracks. Amongst them were Vulcan, Guy, Thornycroft and, most successful of all, Morris, whose half track lorries became the Land-Rovers of their day. Crossley also made half tracks, but these used the rival Kegresse system favoured also by Citroën.

Roadless tracks were supplied to many parts of the world and per-

---

The most unexpected vehicles were converted and here we have an Austin 20 with bodywork designed for a Highlands estate.

---

Quite a well-known vehicle in the technical press of the time was this Super Sentinel Roadless Tractor which appeared in numerous guises, but was always the same vehicle. Some were certainly exported.

formed well. However, by the thirties, four and six wheel drive trucks were able to accomplish much that tracked vehicles could do yet be more practical for road use. Roadless concentrated more and more on tracked agricultural vehicles where these objections caused no problems, and after the 1939-45 war their half track Fordson E27N Majors became a common sight. Later still they developed all wheel drive conversions for tractors and these and their earlier tracked tractors will be described in detail in our forthcoming Farm Machinery Annual.

When Roadless introduced their most famous half track, it overcame the wear problems sometimes encountered with the earlier variety, which lasted for only 25% of their usual life in very dry conditions despite oil filled spherical joints. The archetypal Roadless track was made of rigid girders in which the plates interlocked to form the equivalent of a giant wheel, and these were fitted to many of the famous Royal National Lifeboat Institution FWD launching tractors.

The Roadless track was an ingenious solution to a serious early transport problem and when its usefulness was replaced by all wheel drive (as early as 1927 Philip Johnson whilst selling Roadless tracks in the Sudan had invented run-flat tyres whose treads, not walls, spread out when deflated) its sponsors sensibly moved with the times and put their experience of off-road traction into 4x4, which explains why they are still alive and well today and making several hundred Ford based 4x4 Roadless tractors each year down at their original half track factory in Hounslow.

Famous motoring artist F Gordon Crosby's concept of what might lie in the future. Though tracks did not take to the road, his ideas of styling were remarkably foresighted for a 1922 painting.

An extremely fore-shortened Morris-Commercial of the late twenties. The bolts round the driving wheel are a bit of a mystery, but were perhaps to enlarge its diameter for track tensioning. Note the patent Roadless idea of building the sprocket teeth into the track rather than the drive wheel, which meant that each tooth had minimum driven contact and hence wear.

On trial in the sand dunes at Birkdale near its seaside Southport factory is this two ton 22.4hp Vulcan. The photograph was taken in 1925 and the vehicle could cope with an extra two tons on a trailer or five if a more powerful engine was fitted. Note the neat increase in header tank height.

Back on the sand dunes, but this time in Lima, Peru, not Lancashire. The gents [who bought it in 1926] are from the Public Works Dept and Morris' agents, Alexander Eccles and Co. Two more were sold to the Peruvian War Ministry.

A British built and AEC engined FWD of 1929 re-equipped with the latest variety of Roadless half track in 1945 for the RNLI. The girder tracks formed the equivalent of giant wheels.

528

# TRANSWORLD TRUCK TRIP

**It is always interesting to see what ancient vehicles survive in far-off countries.
In this round-up of photographs from Spain, Greece, South America and
the Indian Ocean, we take a last glimpse at a disappearing mode of transport
as characterless modern light trucks [often Japanese] sweep all before them.
Readers are invited to submit similar shots for future annuals.**

IN the highly industrialised countries
of Western Europe and North
America, the intense pressures of
efficient operation and vehicle laws
make the use of trucks much over ten
years old extremely rare. In more
relaxed warmer climes old vehicles
are coaxed along for many more
years. The lack of cold and damp,
plus corrosive salt in the winter,
ensures that they remain with some-

thing like their original appearance,
even if they have become mechanical
hybrids in the interests of spares
supply.

These photographs were taken in
Spain, Majorca, Athens, the Indian
Ocean Seychelles and Manizales,
Colombia, by Mrs Bart Vanderveen,
Arthur Ingram, Nick Baldwin and
George Avramidis. Despite the
interesting vehicles shown, there is

no doubt that progress is marching
rapidly in these countries and it will
not be long before vehicles more than
ten years old are extinct.

**Bart Vanderveen saw this c1931 Citroën B14
on a 1000km trip down the east coast of
Spain.**

That brilliant and eccentric French car and aircraft designer Voisin was responsible for the little Barcelona built Biscuter. This 'commercial' of the mid-fifties has a 197cc Hispano-Villiers two stroke.

The NAZAR was produced during 1957-65 by Factorias Nápoles SA of Zaragoza [hence the name] whose factory was eventually bought by Barreiros. This early Perkins engined truck now serves as a wrecker. Later production had a revised frontal appearance, with less character.

Spanish made Borgward-ISO Super, with 62 bhp Perkins diesel engine, was one of the products of Borgward ISO Espanola SA in Madrid. It was basically the German Borgward B1500F 1½ tonner.

This, the Sisu and the 1953 Ford bus/truck, were photographed in and around Manizales, a town of 225,000 inhabitants some 2100 metres up in the mountains between Bogota and the West Coast. Most of the sheet metal of this crew-cab truck is 1933 Chevrolet, but the chassis may well be something completely different. A very original 1940 Chevy sedan was also seen.

From 1956, Motor Ibérica in Barcelona [previously the Ford assembly plant] licence-produced the Fordson Thames under the EBRO name. Known as the Model B35 it was available only with EBRO 4 cyl 70 bhp 3610cc diesel engine whereas before V8 petrol and Perkins P6 were used. Wheelbase was 3,85m. There was also a slightly heavier Model B45.

This little stake rack truck could be either a 1941 Ford passenger car fitted with truck cab and body, or a Ford half-tonner with 1941 Ford car front end sheet metal.

The EBRO B35C was a 3 metre wheelbase semi-forward control variant of the Model B35, providing extra cargo space. The stylish front end was a Spanish exclusive.

Opel Blitz dating from 1936/7, with military pattern soft top cab, probably a left-over from the Spanish Civil War. Still powered by its original 6 cyl petrol engine, this would make a most attractive object for restoration and preservation.

Becoming very rare now are Civil War Russian trucks like this ZIS-5. Despite its archaic looks it has probably been dieselised.

Now to Palma, Majorca, where a friend of artist David Shepherd managed to photograph the contents of an old railway yard before it was demolished. As well as an early shunting Fordson tractor and twenties Citroën pickup there was this Renault car converted to flange wheels.

Also in Majorca, Arthur Ingram spotted some interesting scrapyard vehicles. This pickup, alongside a Buick 8, was presumably cut down from a large Hotchkiss car.

An attractive and apparently quite sound c1930 Chevrolet truck awaiting its fate.

German rarity in the shape of a Deutz-engined Kramer left behind by contractors when they had completed Victoria Harbour some twenty years ago. They also left several Magirus-Deutz with minimal mileage but no spares. This, and the Bedford, were seen in the Seychelles, the rest on these two pages in Greece.

A Bedford S type in outstanding condition by British standards but typical of the vehicles in use in the Seychelles. Most 'modern' commercial vehicles are 'threepenny bit' Austins, Land-Rovers and 2-3 ton Japanese trucks.

WWII Chevrolet C30 4x4 used for carrying girders round a construction yard.

Another ex-military vehicle photographed by George Avramidis, this time from the other side. It is a c1940 Mercedes-Benz L3000A, the A signifying all wheel drive and the 3000 its payload in kgs.

A venerable forty year old Dodge tipper more concerned with traction than avoiding skids, judging by the state of its tyres.

In the same yard as the Chevrolet C30 is this familiar Austin K6 6x4 also used as a crane.

A 4x2 Mercedes-Benz L3000 masquerading as a WWII Chevrolet.

Looking remarkably tidy and original is this Austin 10 pickup of WWII origin.

Looking rather American but for its Michelin wheels is this 1933/34 Citroën 'stake truck' alongside an aerodynamic black Peugeot.

A rather unsafe looking bus-cum-truck, its engine room covered by a 1953 Ford passenger car front end. It is one of many contraptions that carry people and goods to market towns from outlying districts, often along roads that are not worthy of the name. This and the Sisu were photographed in Manizales.

Not quite as old as it looks is this Kontio-Sisu K138 dump truck of c1960 of Finnish origin but probably assembled in their thriving South American plant. Other unusual European vehicles included IFA W50L from East Germany and Zastava from Yugoslavia.

We now move back to Athens, where it seems a number of ex-WWII trucks are still earning their living. Note the left-hand drive on this Bedford OXD.

# SHEPPEE & HIS SUPER-HEATED STEAMERS

**Sheppee was one of the leading technical innovators of the steam wagon age whose vehicles were brilliant yet temperamental.
By means of some dedicated research and unequalled knowledge of the industry
R A WHITEHEAD has managed to unearth a story that is as fascinating
as it is important to early history.**

FRANCIS Faulkner Sheppee was born in Poona, India, the son of Francis Sheppee, a surgeon, and his wife, Helen Maria, on 26th June 1833. After education in England, he joined the Army as a cadet on 10th January 1849 and returned to India in March 1852 with a posting to the Artillery in Bombay, one of the areas which remained loyal in the mutiny. After successive promotions, he retired in 1872 with the rank of Major (brevet Lieutenant Colonel), henceforth devoting himself to his business interest (including, *inter alia*, the chairmanship of Exchange Telegraph), his hobbies and his family. The latter must have consumed much of his time for his marriage in 1865 to the nineteen-year-old Alice Jessie Johnstone produced thirteen children, of whom only five survived infancy.

The hobby of his latter years, however, was the development of the steam goods vehicle for use on roads, a subject that had also fascinated his contemporary (though younger) fellow officer, Lieutenant Crompton, who had devoted much time and energy to the promotion of steam road trains as a means of traction in rural India, using road steamers of Thomson's design. Whether or not the two met, or whether Crompton influenced Sheppee is now impossible to say but though, in outline, their objectives had some similarity, their methods were entirely different.

One of the Serpollet cars made, or at least assembled, in the PLT works at York in which Colonel Sheppee had an interest.

Crompton favoured vehicles of robust and relatively simple design, capable of being maintained in remote places with simple facilities. Sheppee, by contrast, was attracted by the work being done in the nineties in France on steam cars and light commercials, notably by Serpollet.

So attracted, in fact, was Sheppee to Serpollet's basis of design that he arranged for Serpollet vehicles to be built under licence at York by the Power, Light & Traction Company, in which he was a shareholder. Although, in the strict sense, an amateur, he had become thoroughly conversant with high pressure steam practice and the merits and shortcomings of flash steam. How far Sheppee controlled PLT is not known, but it was through his association with it that he became acquainted with John E Gibbs, who was an engineer and designer at PLT, and later founded and ran for many years a leading motor garage in York.

In 1902, Sheppee, then seventy years old, withdrew his money from PLT and later in the year the company placed itself in voluntary liquidation. Again we have no evidence as to what was cause and what was effect, but Gibbs withdrew about the same time, buying a house and outbuildings in Thomas Street, York, in which he established himself as an engineer specialising in steam car work. To what extent Colonel Sheppee put up the money for this initial venture is not known, but subsequent events suggest that he, in all probability, provided the necessary funds. It was in this works which Gibbs set up that the vehicles were built in which Sheppee developed his own ideas as to the form which a steam goods carrying vehicle needed to take in order to achieve practical and commercial success. The first was, as we shall see, very nearly attained but the second eluded him completely.

One of the mechanics John Gibbs took with him from PLT to Thomas Street was Tom Notley, who worked for the new company and its successors for the rest of his working life and who lived until 1975. It is very largely because of the interest shown by Tom Notley and the present company that it has been possible to put together the present account of its history.

The initial Thomas Street thinking continued to be on Serpollet principles, though not slavish in detail. The first vehicle built there was a light lorry of perhaps a ton to thirty hundredweight load capacity with the boiler rear mounted and liquid fired in true Serpollet fashion. No photographs of it are known to survive and, as the works drawings were discarded during

No picture exists of the first wagon built at Thomas Street but this is the second, with the boiler transferred to the front. Still of very light construction, it probably carried about a ton and had a rear-mounted condenser.

the 1939-45 war, the information concerning it is derived from Tom Notley. After the lorry had been tested, it was found not to satisfy Col Sheppee and, accordingly, a second wagon was constructed, this time with the boiler mounted at the front. To what extent the boiler and other components were modified is not clear - the problems which John Gibbs and his men were tackling under Col Sheppee's supervision were those involved in the generation and use of flash steam at relatively high superheat and in the elimination of manual regulation of water and fuel supplies. There seems to have been no experiment with the type of fuel - from first to last this was kerosene. This second vehicle likewise failed to fulfil its creator's exacting standards and yet another was built to take its place. These first three wagons represent the purely experimental phase of the firm's activities. It is doubtful indeed if they were co-existent.

At the end of the experiments with the second wagon, if not before, Col Sheppee discarded the Serpollet boiler, substituting a flash boiler of his own, or Gibbs' design, made by Tom Notley. This first true Sheppee boiler consisted of horizontal banks, approximately square on plan, of solid drawn seamless tube, each coupled to the next at inlet and outlet by a short 'D' connection of similar tube with a union at each end. This was used in a third and a fourth vehicle, each again of about thirty hundredweight carrying capacity. These two lorries were stiffened-up versions of the second, but several chassis components as well as the front wheels, axle and suspension appear to have been carried forward from one to the next. It may well be that a good many minor parts also carried forward. Heavier rear wheels with twin solid tyres were used in the two later versions and the condenser

The third wagon made was a heavier version of number two, the fuel tank still under the cab but with vertical tube condensers front mounted on either side the boiler and twin rear wheels. Some components of the older wagons were re-used but much was new.

Wagon four was a less drastic rebuild and the changes were mainly in the boiler but in addition the fuel tank had been removed to the rear and a heavier driving chain had been used.

When is a rebuild a new vehicle?
This is a heavily rebuilt version of
wagon four.

The Sheppee stand at the Olympia
Show in 1907.

was arranged in two banks
flanking the boiler casing on near
and off sides, whilst in all three a
vertical central chimney was
used. The engine used in at least
the two latter of these four
vehicles was a breakaway from
Serpollet lines, using a pair of
double acting high pressure
cylinders with poppet valves.
The rear axle was driven by a
roller chain and incorporated the
differential.

As a result of the experiments
with the boilers of these lorries,
the final form of the Sheppee
steam generator was developed
consisting of coils totalling 300
linear feet of solid drawn seamless tube, arranged in ten horizontal rectangular layers, each
coupled to the next by the same
type of short 'D' shaped connections with a union each end as
before and finished off with a
square coil at the base. The front
and back of the boiler was
formed of ten steel drums
similarly coupled. Water entered
one of the lowest pair of steel
drums, passing successively
through each to the top whence
it was taken by a long connection back to the square base coil
rising through this and the two
rectangular coils above it. It was
then taken by another long
connection to the top coil and
circulated downwards through
the rectangular coils to the third
from the bottom, known as the
steam coil from whence it
emerged as superheated steam
into the main steam pipe and
thence to the throttle valve. By
permutations of the 'D' couplings, however, the route
through the coils could be varied
very considerably and, though
the one noted above was a
common one and was, indeed,
one of two entered in the
instruction handbook, others
were employed from time to
time, especially in experiments.

The lower coils and the drums
were wound with piano wire,
under Sheppee's own patent, to
increase their resistance to heat
and pressure. The tube forming
the coil was wound with wire in
a hollow mandrel lathe before
bending to provide reinforce-
ment against the pressures
aimed at, which were of the
order of 400/500 psi, with very
high superheat.

Except for William Foden,
who was developing his overtype steam wagon design with a
compound engine mounted on
the locomotive type boiler and a
long chain drive to the rear axle,
virtually all other contemporary
British designers and experi-
menters were concentrating on
vertical boilers coupled to a
compound engine mounted
beneath the chassis. These latter
produced wagons that either
rated as failures or had very

limited success from three main
contributory causes, namely,
that in consequence of the low
pressures employed (mostly
200 psi or less), the virtual
absence of effective superheat
and the long and unprotected
path of the steam delivery pipe
from boiler to engine, the latter
received steam that was wet,
reduced in pressure and often,
because of the limited steaming
capacity of the boiler, restricted
in quantity. The Sentinel, six
years later, with its generous
boiler capacity, effective super-
heater and large double cylin-
dered engine, was the first
thoroughly practicable undertype, but its very empiricism
would have made it anathema to
Sheppee, convinced that the
future of road transport lay with
the fast, relatively light vehicle.

Sheppee did not, in the event,
solve entirely the problems of his
flash steam generator and its
controls to the point where the
resultant vehicle was a truly
satisfactory day-to-day performer in the hands of a steam
wagon driver of ordinary skills
though he did produce a series
of vehicles which, when driven
by his factory trained men,
produced remarkable results for
their time.

By keeping both the laden and
unladen weights low, he was
able to use solid rubber tyres
from the beginning, which gave
him an advantage both in road
speeds and resistance to shocks.
Ackermann steering was used in
the early experimental models
and all subsequent vehicles. The
design of the engine in the two
earliest experimental vehicles

may have been pure Serpollet
but for their successor Sheppee
and Gibbs produced what was,
with variations of detail, to be
their standard design. The term
standard' has to be used with
some circumspection as, like
Doble after them, they could
never bring themselves to
consider any point of design as
stabilised for a production run
and, in consequence, no two
vehicles they made were exactly
alike, though, in essence, they
were similar.

The experiments with the four
early lorries had consumed some
two years and resulted in a new
design, a short wheelbase lorry
of about 1 ½ tons load capacity,
convertible, by an exchange of
body, to a charabanc. The
Sheppee flash boiler was placed
at the front of the chassis with a
gilled tube condenser having an
aluminium alloy top tank but
open sides, closely resembling
the radiator of a petrol vehicle,
placed at the leading end. On
this tank the firm used, probably
for the first time, its trademark,
consisting of a piston ring
bearing crossed mushroom
valves. The power unit placed
amidships under the chassis was
a four cylinder poppet valved
engine of their own design,
which will be dealt with in detail
later on in this article, assembled
from comparatively small
components using high tensile
bolts, a point made much of as a
virtue in catalogues and
advertising. The makers claimed
that it made the engine
extremely accessible and the
renewing of components easy -
a point which is likely to be
disputed by anyone with experience of trying, in a confined
space, to undo steel nuts which
have had lengthy exposure to
heat - which may be a case of
making a virtue of necessity as it
is at least likely that the designers made individual components
small so as to keep them within
the capacity of the works which,
though usefully equipped, was
on a small scale compared with
the major steam engine builders.
The lorry also seems to have
been fitted, like the fourth
experimental vehicle, with a
supplementary coil condenser at
the rear, a feature not perpetu-
ated in subsequent designs.
Indeed, this feature, together
with a marked similarity between
the underworks of this lorry and
the fourth experimental lorry
suggest that it may have been, in
effect, yet another rebuild. One
cannot be sure.

This lorry was taken on a test
run up Sutton Bank, a steep hill
with a hairpin bend near the
foot, between Thirsk and Helms-
ley over which many Sheppee
tests were conducted. The
maximum grade was about 1 in
3.9. In a little under a mile the
road rose six hundred feet, an
average rise of the order of 1 in
8. The run accomplished was
about 40 miles beginning at York
and ending, involuntarily with a
broken crankshaft, at Oswaldkirk. Colonel Sheppee's son
Francis went on the trip with

Reputedly a picture of the un-scheduled stop at Oswaldkirk when the crankshaft broke on the test run. The lady in the large hat, on the rear seat, is obviously wondering why she ever agreed to come on the trip. A condenser is still mounted between the rear axle and the fuel tank but an open sided condenser bank with top tank is placed at the front in the 'radiator' position.

The first vehicle sold by Sheppee was a rather heavier vehicle bought by Moore & Sharp, haulage contractors of Ovenden, Halifax. In this illustration it is shown with a demountable charabanc body.

Pledger and Cornner, the two works drivers, and the report of the trip, set out in the table is interesting.

At the end of the report a manuscript footnote was added, 'Stop after stop No 6 on steepest part of Sutton Bank. Lorry got over steep part and was then stopped for 3 minutes to look around and examine generally.

'Stop, after stop mentioned above, on top of Sutton Bank to wait while passengers walked up. Owing to stoutness and scantiness of health of some of these, this stop extended over ¼ hour to 20 minutes. These two stops not noted so are put in here.'

The body carried for this trip was a light demountable chara-banc with six banks of seats.
There is a photograph extant of either this vehicle or another of similar characteristics, including the open sided gilled conden-ser, taken inside the works but the background has been partially obliterated to prepare the photograph for use in publicity material. A further and rather heavier version was built capable probably of taking a three ton payload and generally more developed in details. In this the condenser was closed in at the sides and the general appear-ance was made more spruce and finished. In this the designers had arrived at the design which, over the next five or six years, the company made a sustained, though largely fruitless, effort to sell. Dimensionally and in matters of detailed construction and assembly successive vehicles continued to differ but the basic layout was not changed.

This lorry was sold to Moore & Sharp, haulage contractors at Ovenden, Halifax. The driver was trained at the works and the lorry was believed by Tom Notley to have lasted up to the 1914 war. What ended its career, in all probability, was that its owners could not be bothered any longer to humour its foibles - the burner cleaning, tube changing, coil purging and other

matters that had to be done thoroughly and regularly to get good work out of it.
As a spin-off from the central problems of design, Gibbs and the Sheppees (father and son) had produced a very compact and serviceable steam driven boiler feed pump and designs of valves for superheated steam which were offered for sale to the trade and public. Quite a useful trade was developed in these components and it was of sufficient importance for the firm to take a stand (No 275) at Olympia in 1907 for the purpose of promoting their sales. Income was further supplemented by the undertaking of repairs to steam and petrol cars and as late as December 1909, when Serpol-let's cars, after his death, were passing rapidly out of fashion,

the Sheppee Motor Company deemed it worthwhile to adver-tise, in *The Autocar*, their services as repairers of Serpollet cars. As many of their men had come from PLT their collective experience of work on the Serpollet marque was probably unrivalled in the country.
How the business at Thomas Street was described in its first days is not known but quite soon it became known as the Sheppee Motor Company with the Sheppees as the major, if not only, partners and it is certainly by this title that it was known well before 1907. How it fared in the commercial promotion of its products will be examined below.
The image of the commercial vehicle constructed on what may be called 'steam car' prin-

ciples, never robust in Britain, sustained a setback from the failure of the Darracq Serpollet steam vehicles owned in London by the Metropolitan Steam Omnibus Company to perform as well as the General's motor buses.
Nevertheless, compared with an overtype or conventional undertype steam wagon, the prizes which a successful design would have brought to its manu-facturer were sufficient to encourage perseverance with the problems. Lower tare weight, greater range between water stops, freedom from risk (however slight) of explosion, silence and great flexibility were the lures by which the flash steam commercial tempted its followers after it. Clarkson pursued the dream longest and

came nearest to success, but Sheppee was close behind and other contenders included Lifu, Fawcett-Fowler, Leyland and SM.

By the time of the sale of the three tonner to Moore & Sharp in 1910, the design of the engine and auxiliaries had been, more or less, stabilised. Certainly, as far as Tom Notley remembered, there was no repetition of the crankshaft fiasco which had terminated the trial run at Oswaldkirk. The firm put in hand the construction of at least two further vehicles resembling the Moore & Sharp lorry in the expectation that buyers would be forthcoming. In dealing with the story of vehicles, such as these, which were not sold, it is difficult to say which were entirely new and which were rebuilds of earlier ones, but certainly at least two of these short wheelbase chassis, used either as trucks or charabancs by demountable bodies, existed concurrently. They are distinguishable in photographs by the fact that one, like the Moore & Sharp example, had a round tie bar between the dumb irons and the other did not. Despite considerable advertising in *Commercial Motor*, *Steam Car Owner* and other periodicals, it proved impossible to sell these two lorries, in part because of the lack of trust hauliers placed in flash steam but also from the limited platform area of the lorries and the fact that their steam generators were of slightly too small capacity.

They spent several years, therefore, in their maker's ownership during which time they were hired out as charabancs, achieving some local popularity because of their quietness and lack of objectionable smell and, from time to time, as lorries. One of the uses to which they were put, as works hacks, was fetching in and returning

cars sent to Thomas Street for repair, particularly cars disabled in accidents.

The Sheppees were well known as businessmen in York and on good terms with many of those who held prominent positions in local industry or in civic affairs. Colonel Sheppee's business interests were centred mainly on the City of London and his residence was in Surrey, but Francis Sheppee had his home at 46 Queen Anne's Road, York, and was closely involved and well known in business and social circles in the area. One of the minor privileges that came from the regard in which they were held was that of using the roads at York Racecourse as a trial ground for wagons. The maximum speed achieved by an unladen wagon on test there was about 40 mph, a remarkable achievement for a commercial in the first decade of this century and, unfortunately, an accomplishment that was of no great practical use. Riding at that speed on a high and unenclosed seat, without a windscreen, was an exhilarating experience. As Tom Notley remarked, it made one hold on. Concurrently with these two lorries, the firm seem to have retained the earlier one with the open-sided vertical tube front condenser which continued to be portrayed in advertisements, one of which

35 H.P. "Sheppee" Steam Car.

One of the pair of lorries supplied to the Tadcaster Tower Brewery Co Ltd in 1912.

---

The wagon supplied to Natal in 1910.

---

One of the duties of the works wagon was to fetch in damaged or disabled cars to the works for repair. The AC two seater here shown being given a lift appears to have lost the nearside stub axle.

---

Forster Coverdale & Co Ltd of Durham, York and Scarborough owned a Sheppee which was used for mineral water deliveries around York.

appeared in *Commercial Motor* during March 1910.

The availability of the Sheppee lorries for hire was made use of, from time to time, by the local brewers and mineral water makers to cope with the seasonal peaks of their respective trades. Forster Coverdale, a mineral water firm with premises in York, often hired the lorries, as did the Tadcaster Tower brewery and Bowmans, the York furniture removers, and the practical experience gained in working for them was used in the development of the third generation of Sheppee wagons.

Unfortunately, because of the destruction of the drawings, the dimensional variations, if any, made in the engine are lost. Tom Notley recalled that the problems were not, on the whole, encountered in the engine but in the burners and vaporisers and in the flash boiler itself. Wooden wheels also required careful attention, especially in hot, dry weather, during which wet sacks would be hung over them when not in use, to keep the woodwork from drying out. The firm's preoccupation was with the steam generator and its appurtenances tended to divert its attention away from such mundane matters as wheels which, in any case, came from outside suppliers, but in 1910 it was fortunate enough to secure from the Ministry of Agriculture in Natal an order for a wagon convertible to a charabanc, for which purpose wooden wheels would have been at a distinct disadvantage and for which, for the first time, cast steel wheels were used. Wheels apart, the wagon supplied was basically similar to the two works wagons but had a higher ground clearance.

Though the main stream of development continued to be on commercials, other work was not neglected. The Sheppees, father and son, must have been carrying on the Thomas Street business largely as an extended experiment but every endeavour was used to conduct it as an economic proposition as far as possible. Repair work to steam cars was canvassed vigorously and auxiliaries such as valves and mountings were sold. Among the more notable of the spin-off manufactures was the Sheppee chain for assisting the

grip of twin solid tyres on greasy, snowy or icy roads, an ingenious device better illustrated than described which enjoyed a limited sale in the years before the outbreak of the war during which thousands of sets were supplied, mostly for military use.

Besides these products, the firm made at least one boiler and engine for a yacht, said to have belonged to a friend of the family and to have been kept in the Solent, and three cars. The earliest was a 35hp tourer with Cape cart hood, and the second was a 25hp with a torpedo cabriolet body which carried the registration number DN392. Of the third, little is known, though it appears in a works photograph in chassis form, generally similar to DN392 but with a much larger and higher front mounted condenser. The cabriolet was certainly used by the Sheppees. Possibly the other two were sold but the consensus of opinion at the works ten years ago was that they, too, were kept for use by the family and firm. Interest in steam cars had taken a distinct downturn by the time the cars were made (1908-11) and it is, therefore, not improbable that they proved unsaleable.

There was also in circulation about that time a third wagon-cum-charabanc generally similar to the wagon for Natal, on cast steel wheels but with eight spokes in the front wheel compared with six in the Natal wagon. Possibly it was the first version of the Natal wagon and was modified before despatch, or it may have been a completely distinct wagon for another, but unnamed, purchaser.

The next wagon was an updated version of the chassis used under the works charabancs, somewhat longer in the chassis but on wooden wheels. According to Tom Notley, once the use of steel wheels had begun the firm offered, for a while, to supply wagons on wooden or cast steel wheels according to the purchaser's preferences. This wagon, dating from about 1911, was on the works strength for some three years but in the last known photograph of it carried the name Forster Coverdale & Co along the chock rail, though whether it was merely on contract hire to them or had been sold outright cannot now be determined. Two wagons broadly of this type were supplied to Tadcaster Tower Brewery Co Ltd in 1912. These were supplied with a fixed roof over the driver but no windscreen. How they performed is not known but there were no repeat orders.

Thereafter, the design of wagons underwent some further minor amendments emerging as what was known as the H type. The chassis was extended a little more, the differential was moved to the intermediate shaft, double chains replaced the single chain, the seat was altered somewhat and cast steel wheels, Y-spoked

Besides owning a wagon, Forster Coverdale were regular hirers of the works wagons. Here one is shown at the end of Thomas Street when on hire to them.

Another regular hirer was the firm of Bowman & Co of York.

An older works wagon [on wooden wheels] working on hire to Forster Coverdale in the early days of the war delivering mineral waters to a military canteen in York. They seem later to have bought this wagon as it appeared lettered in their name.

The one and only 'Overseas Special' photographed at York racecourse with its attendant pole truck.

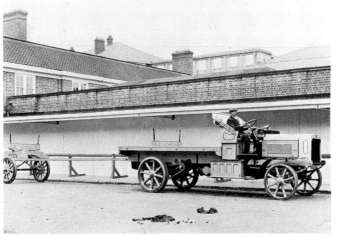

at the rear, were adopted as standard. At least three were made of this design, one of which went to Forster Coverdale, the other two being used for hire in York. This design was further developed into what the firm called the 'Overseas Special' in which, by the use of larger wheels and appropriate amendments to the suspension, they secured an 18ins ground clearance. In 1913 they supplied a wagon of this type to the Venezuelan Government Railways, complete with a pole attachment to enable it to carry telephone poles or railway lines. Whether the design was evolved to meet the enquiry, or whether the former attracted the latter, cannot now be determined. The wagon was tested on York racecourse and upon Sutton Bank, before being crated up and despatched, together with a massive supply of spares, whereafter nothing more was heard of it. Rumour has it that one further such wagon was made and sent to Karachi. Tom Notley prefaced his recollection of this by the words 'I believe'. He had a wonderful memory and it must, therefore, be counted a strong probability but not a certainty.

There was also in circulation about this time a further wagon with a rather wider condenser without the aluminium alloy side columns. This may have been an entirely new vehicle or an experiment with one of the existing works fleet. The total score, including the two cars, was thus of the order of twenty vehicles, of which no more than eight, and possibly only six, found commercial buyers.

By the time war broke out in 1914, Colonel Sheppee was eighty-one - an advanced age, even for a very remarkable man, at which to be the force behind a continuing series of experiments. For a while, in the strange period of the autumn of 1914, when many believed that the numerical superiority of the Allies was such as to ensure the defeat of the Central Powers by Christmas 1914, things went on much as before at Thomas Street. The works wagons were in demand for hire and carried *inter alia* beer and mineral waters for the Territorials and other troops mustered in York, but, as

the war situation degenerated into stalemate in 1915 and the scandal of the munitions shortage became evident, matters changed. Further development work was shelved, and the Thomas Street works took up munitions contracts. Colonel Sheppee died in 1917 and with him the last chance of there being any perseverance with the promotion of flash steam lorries. Aside from any other consideration, the financial position had changed in a dramatic fashion. Though the works had been well run and every endeavour had been made to make it commercially viable, the fact remained that it had depended upon Colonel Sheppee to contribute sizeable annual sums to the cost of research. The war finished this, in part by reason of the diminution - because of inflation - of the value of Col Sheppee's personal resources, and in part, after his death, by the redistribution of them under the terms of his will. All this apart, had his son, Frank Sheppee, inherited the whole estate intact, at pre-war levels of value, there is no indication that he would have continued to run Thomas Street as, in effect, the hobby of a well-to-do man. He must have realised how slim, by then, were the chances of promoting the sophisticated flash-steam commercial against the petrol engined competition by which it was already outnumbered by several thousand to one or, in the field still open to steam, against what had, by then, become conventional overtypes and undertypes.

For some two years after the death of his father, Frank Sheppee carried on the firm as a private venture, mostly undertaking high class jobbing engineering. It must be remembered that the works had an irreproachable name in York for the quality of the finished work it produced and this, coupled with the fact that Frank Sheppee was a director also of National Glass Works (York) Ltd, North Eastern Paper Mills Ltd and of the York Engineering & Foundry Co Ltd, provided it with a steady flow of work when war production came to an end. In August 1919, however, it was incorporated as a limited liability company, the Sheppee Motor Co Ltd, with a nominal capital of £30,000 in £1 shares and with Frank Sheppee and his son-in-law, Alfred Furlong, a barrister of Tolworth, Surrey, as directors. A E Miethe became the secretary. Four years later, John Charles Stapleton of Acomb, York - an engineer - also joined the board. Under the constitution of the company, Frank Sheppee was to be the governing director until he died or until he chose to relinquish the post, and he was the owner of all but two of the shares, the other two being the qualifying shares held by his fellow directors.

Some debate is said to have taken place as to whether the steam vehicles were to be finally abandoned but the question had

An H class chassis outside the works in Thomas Street. The aluminium chain case behind the chain sprocket of the final drive housed the primary chain between the crankshaft and countershaft. In the early wagons which were shorter in the chassis, the two were geared together but later wagons had a primary chain drive. Not only did it suit the length of the wagon better but also helped to take up chassis flexing which tended to cause gear binding in the earlier wagons.

Three wagons on York racecourse - an H type leading, followed by a slightly earlier version on wooden wheels, whilst bringing up the rear is the mysterious wagon with wider condenser without side panels.

been virtually decided by events and was almost a foregone conclusion. There was also a tentative proposal to take up a licence to make or assemble the French De Dion motor lorry but even at a time when the British commercial vehicle industry still contained many firms trading on a limited scale, Sheppee would have been smaller than most, whilst to have increased the scale would have meant a move from the compact and well organised works. In the end, the project that was settled upon was a motor assisted bicycle, dubbed the 'Cykelaid', a machine which performed well in Speed Trials and ACU tests, but which failed to achieve large scale sales, mainly because, with its limited production runs and high standard of workmanship and materials, it was dear enough to limit its market. By the end of the twenties, in fact, it had been overtaken in price by the cheaper full size mass-produced motor cycles and production had to be given up, a fate which also overtook a very advanced domestic washing machine and powered wringer, designed and marketed in the same period.

In February 1926 the freehold, plant and chattels of the firm were mortgaged to the Midland Bank Limited to guarantee the firm's account, and eighteen months later £4500 worth of 5% debentures were created and issued. As the hopes of the future of the Cykelaid and the washing machines faded, the company took up the work which was soon to form its staple product, namely, machinery for the glass bottle trade. In 1930, Frank Sheppee sold 4000 of his shares to Stapleton, 3000 to Miethe and 4000 to a newcomer, S G Jowitt. The slump was, however, imminent and business declined, so that in April 1932 the directors took the decision to place the old company in voluntary liquidation for the purpose of reconstruction, Alfred Miethe and a man named Arthur Barron, the company's accountant, being appointed liquidators.

From them, the present company bought the business and premises complete, as a going concern, trading as the Sheppee Motor & Engineering

Co Ltd, recently contracted to Sheppee Engineering Ltd, and concentrating upon the production of machinery for bottle-makers, principally loaders for annealing ovens. The board of the new company were the shareholders and directors of its predecessor. Frank Sheppee, who continued to be governing director in the new company, died in August 1960, having outlived, by sixteen months, Samuel Jowitt. Alfred Miethe was, for many years, secretary to the present company, but Arthur Barron died in 1939. Notwithstanding these few changes in ownership of shares and the boardroom structure of the company, they passed almost unnoticed in the works and life there remained very stable over the years, with continuity of employment of individuals extending to thirty, forty or, in cases such as Tom Notley's, over fifty years and great mutual regard between men and management. Though the plant policy has been very progressive, the buildings and surroundings have not been the subject of drastic change and many of the backdrops of the photographs of seventy years ago may still be seen. There is

also a continuing interest in the vehicles which caused the firm to be founded.

Since Tom Notley died, no one is left alive who had close contact with the making and running of the early lorries. He used to divide the steam lorry (or 'lorrie' as Sheppee spelled the word) period into two parts, the prelimary or experimental period - up to 1909 - and the production period (1910-14) when sales were canvassed, catalogues prepared and issued and, for the size of firm, extensive advertising undertaken. Elaborate and well-produced manuals and catalogues were issued for the H type and Overseas Special wagons commensurate with a firm many times the size of Sheppee and with sales vastly in excess of those actually achieved. Why then did the wagons fail to catch on and why were there no repeat orders? The answer is at least twofold. The first part concerns consistency and type of performance. The Venezuelan wagon, on test, did twenty miles an hour fully loaded at York racecourse and could have sustained the speed (other factors apart) for hours since the rate of gener-

ation of steam did not depend on thermal reserve in the boiler but on the regular pumping of matched quantities of paraffin and water to the burner and steam generator respectively. This cannot be described as other than a very considerable achievement. On the other hand, it was of very little use to a contemporary haulier in day-to-day work. Moreover, the Sheppee wagons were beset by unpredictable quirks of behaviour, mostly springing from burner clogging, so that one day, or perhaps for several days running, the generator would produce copious supplies of steam with complete reliability yet would follow it with a day when nothing would go right and when the burner would clog time after time, producing luminous flames and far too little heat.

The second facet of the failure to achieve success was perhaps as follows. Driving a Sheppee wagon when it was running well could be relatively simple, but the simplicity was achieved at the expense of comparatively sophisticated lighting up and preparation procedures and complicated technology in the manufacture and maintenance.

**A useful by-product of Sheppee ingenuity - the Sheppee chain. To prevent the chain remaining still whilst the wheel revolved the end of the chain formed a loop round the rim of the wheel.**

The reverse was the case with an overtype steam wagon such as a Foden or a Garrett. The underlying technology was relatively simple but it required continuous manual management on the road - firing up, maintaining the water level in the boiler and selection of gear ratios. The maintenance and driving of an overtype wagon conformed more with the bank of experience built up with traction engines than with steam car type techniques of which hauliers and their drivers were suspicious. The Foden or the Garrett was a consistent performer, day by day and week by week. The Sheppee tended to be brilliant and temperamental by turns which, on the whole, customers in 1911-13 found tiresome. They could get the same type of erratic behaviour from petrol engined contemporaries without the additional worries of water supplies or flash generators. When a Sheppee misbehaved on the road it was usually possible to do something on the spot that would enable it to reach home, but this might involve rearranging the D connectors to bypass a burned out steam coil, cleaning out a vaporiser coil or dismantling and refitting the burner, jobs that required a fair set of tools and the skills of a mechanic. As Tom Notley said, in the words quoted earlier on, every time the firm built a wagon it had to build a driver to go with it. In many respects this was harder than making the wagon.

In talking about his days with the Sheppee steam lorries, Tom Notley used to come back again and again to the unsolved problems of the steam generators and their attendant burners. At any rate in the H class lorries and Overseas Specials, offered commercially, the engines, transmission systems, wheels, axles, springs and chassis needed relatively little attention - less, in his opinion, than those of the general run of motor lorries of the period - but steam coils and burners were another matter and to understand a little more clearly why this should have been the case, it may be worth looking at the burner construction in detail.

The construction of the burner was basically a sheet steel box containing a flame plate of small cast iron slotted members secured by screws. On top of these members there was the main vaporiser coil - three sections of solid drawn seamless steel tube ending in the steel main nipple. At the side of the nipple, pointing up the sheet steel induction tube there was a gas nut - a tapered snout drilled with four small holes for the issue of the vaporised fuel. A blank nut for cleaning was screwed on to the nipple

opposite the end of the vaporiser. The action was thus almost exactly a parallel with that of a paraffin blowlamp and prone to all the same troubles. It could work like a charm all one day and it could be a complete pig for the whole of the next. Dirty paraffin could carbon up the gas orifices or scale from inside the vaporiser tube could block them. Sometimes pricking or reamering out the holes was enough but often the gas nut and its blank opposite had to be taken out to clean the nipple. If the vaporiser itself was seriously choked, it had to be removed from the burner and blown out with steam. The recommended method was to connect one end to a boiler force pump and to heat the vaporiser well in a forge fire, tapping it to loosen the scale. When the coil was well heated, a little water was pumped in which, flashing into steam, blew out the dirt. It was a good idea to stand clear of the free end whilst this was being done. A somewhat similar method was recommended for clearing blocked boiler coils. Another method was to substitute a spare vaporiser, raise steam in the engine and connect the blocked vaporiser to one of the plugged openings in the steam end of the donkey pump. On opening the donkey pump throttle valve, the tube could be blown through with boiler steam.

Since the main burner was not needed to be burning the whole time, it was necessary to provide a pilot burner to keep the main vaporiser at working temperature when the main flame was off and also to provide a flame for igniting it when required. This pilot was placed at the nearside front of the main burner casing and on the opposite side of the casing an inspection door was provided in which there was a mica vision panel. The pilot consisted of a cylindrical slotted steel flame plate fitting over the end of a horizontal induction tube with a rectangular vaporiser having cleaning plugs at the corners and a single holed jet with a needle valve for regulating the size of the flame. The nipple had cleaning nuts at the bottom and sides. A slot in the pilot flame plate located on to a peg on the main burner and the pilot was protected from the cold air by a sheet steel shield attached by a wing nut. The ends and nipples of both main and pilot vaporisers were lagged with asbestos.

The slots in the main and pilot flame plates were 1/32ins wide and the dimension was critical, deviation causing back fires in the burner and a flare-up which, though sometimes spectacular, was rarely dangerous. Partially blocked slots could be righted with a hacksaw blade but an oversize one had to be corrected with asbestos paste - a far less effective remedy. A sign of burner unrest was a whistling or hooting noise, caused either by excessive pressure - over about 75 lbs per sq in - in the paraffin

The Cykelaid applied to an elderly gentleman's tricycle. The rider of a conventional trike needs skill. One wonders what the extra weight at the front did for it.

The launch engine built by Sheppee

The supplementary brake drum attached to later Cykelaids.

receiver or by a main vaporiser that was not hot enough, a defect caused by starting it too soon after lighting up the pilot or, if the noise developed on the road, by blocking of the pilot jet and consequent reduction of the pilot flame, or again by dirt in the main jets or flame plates.

The procedure on lighting up was firstly to light the blow lamp provided with the lorry. This was arranged to play through the door provided in the side of the burner box onto the pilot vaporiser until this was hot enough to vaporise the paraffin fuel. The paraffin valve of the pilot was then turned on, setting the pilot flame going which, in its turn, played upon the main vaporiser. After four or five minutes of heating, the main burner was ready for ignition. First the bypass valve on the paraffin line was closed, sending the fuel route through the automatic controls, after which the second paraffin valve was gently opened and closed once or twice until the main burner was burning with a clear even flame. Once the driver was satisfied that the burner was working properly, he could turn the main burner off until required and, in the meantime, attend to the lubrication.

Sheppee would supply engine and cylinder lubricating oils of a grade to withstand the degree of superheat encountered in their engines and, according to Tom Notley, these gave reasonable satisfaction. Lubrication of the cylinders was by a mechanical lubricator into the steam line by the throttle valve. Understandably, the inlet valves were the most vulnerable and one wonders how well they would have stood up to continuous running at high speeds or at maximum pressure. Lubrication of other parts followed, in the main, motor practice. The oiling of the engine was attended to by a second mechanical lubricator, which pumped oil to the big ends, gudgeon pins and side bearings of the crankshaft.

In the closing stages of the lubrication routine, the main burner was given another shorter run of three or four minutes to warm the boiler through, after which it was turned off and the pilot regulated ready for the road. The main burner was then relit and if the steam pressure had not risen after a minute or so, some water was pumped into the boiler by hand using the donkey pump hand lever until there was enough pressure to work it by steam. The pet cock on the pump was briefly opened to release any trapped air and then, as soon as pressure reached

300 lbs, the engine was ready for starting, the cylinder drain cocks being first opened to release any condensate. The lorry was moved a few inches forward and back several times and finally drawn out of the garage in full forward gear with the cocks still open. After some thirty yards, the drain cocks were closed and the reverser was gradually brought back to the notched-up or running position. During all these proceedings, water was supplied to the boiler by the donkey pump, but once the lorry was properly in motion the donkey was shut off and the fuel and water was regulated entirely by the automatic controls. If the lorry was slowed for traffic or for a sharp bend, the reverser had to be put to the full forward position briefly before being notched up again. For normal running, the steam pressure required was about 300 lbs per square inch.

The makers recommended, contrary to modern practice, the use of the hand brake for ordinary braking and the transmission brake on the countershaft, worked by the foot pedal, only for emergencies. As a third brake, the reverser could be used with the throttle closed.

The donkey pump was intended for the generation of extra steam for hill climbing and other exceptional demands. By its means, additional water could be introduced into the boiler coil and it would normally start only on a pressure of 400 psi or more. To start it, the foot was lifted a little on the main throttle pedal and the donkey throttle valve, a star wheel on the steering column, was gently opened. Thus, the use of the donkey required a certain amount of intelligent anticipation as it had to be set in motion before the lorry had begun to climb, a requirement not very difficult to

Off to tennis at the vicarage on a Cykelaid assisted bicycle. Braking by ordinary cycle brakes was the weakest point of the system and later a supplementary rear wheel brake attached to the spokes was designed.

---

An early H type posed outside the works *c*1912.

---

The footplate of an H type. On the right are the handbrake and donkey pump hand lever. The star handle in the foreground controls the fuel by-pass valve and that on the steering column the donkey pump steam. The large lever on the column is the reversing lever. The foot pedals are brake and throttle respectively. The left hand top gauge on the scuttle shows air pressure in the paraffin receiver and that on the right, steam pressure. The lower gauge is for the bearings lubricator. The spring loaded foot pedal works the warning gong. Behind it are the cylinder drain cock foot pedal and the emergency hand throttle valve wheel. The small handle above the reversing lever controls the by-pass on the pump line. The indicator on the scuttle below the gauges indicates the pyrometer reading.

The donkey pump with the outer boxing open. On the extreme right is a mechanical lubricator.

fulfil on roads familiar to the driver but rather harder when he was on strange territory.

The lorry was intended to run at about 300 psi with the use of higher pressures for hill climbing - up to 800 psi - at which pressure the driver was recommended to use the relief valve to reduce pressure, or at least prevent any further rise. After a long hill climb, the boiler would get very hot and on passing the summit the pressure would shoot up, necessitating the use of the relief valve, which otherwise was not much required.

The working temperature of the boiler was 800-850° F, sufficient to give the main steam pipe a glow in complete darkness. Great stress was laid on the need to keep the boiler close to this temperature - too much heat damaged the coils and too little made the engine run badly. The pyrometer was one of Sheppee's ingenious and effective devices, a long D tube that projected from the boiler and acted on the heel of a lever placed behind the dashboard. The upper end of the lever was formed into a small rack which meshed with a pinion which, in turn, caused a pointer to move over the face of a dial in front of the driver just below the steam and air pressure gauges. A projection on the lever passed through the dashboard and pressed against the tappet of a valve fitted on the dashboard and attached to the paraffin supply pipe. Expansion of the D tube on excessive heating caused the lever to move forward, pushing home the valve and decreasing the flow of paraffin.

The second automatic control was a pressure cut-out. A spring loaded piston worked in a small cylinder against boiler pressure. Excess pressure depressed the piston, the tail-rod of which pushed down the tappet of the paraffin valve, shutting off the supply. An adjustment on the tappet regulated cut off in relation to boiler pressure. Both regulators worked on the same valve and both were under the driver's eye.

Despite the automatic devices the driver's task could be exacting. Besides steering and regulating speed with the throttle and brakes, he had to watch the steam and air pressure gauges and the pyrometer, and to keep an eye open for anything likely to increase the demand for steam so that the donkey pump could be brought into action in good time. All these things were simple in themselves, once understood, and involved no great physical exertion save, perhaps, in the steering. In addition to these points, however, he had to be a good enough mechanic to clear blocked burners, remove burned out boiler coils and carry out the other items of running maintenance the demanding machine called for. Each completed wagon was tested with full load upon Sutton Bank, a 1¼ mile slope of 1 in 4 maximum gradient which occurred on a hairpin.

By way of compensation for these requirements, however, the driver never had the drudgery of humping coal, emptying the ashpan, clinkering off or, in the conventional sense, washing out the boiler, nor was the lorry demanding in water because of the economy brought about by its being fully condensing.

The exhaust steam from both engine and donkey were taken through the feed water heater, a plain galvanised drum enclosing the water feed pipe. The drum had a pressure relief valve to

prevent undesirable back pressures. After leaving the feed water heater, the steam passed through the condenser, a bank of gilled tubes and two headers mounted in the place occupied by the radiator of an i.c. lorry and from thence the condensate was taken back to the tank. The condenser was mounted on the chassis by linked couplings designed to relieve it of chassis stresses and to accommodate expansion. The condensing system enabled a wagon to cover 25 or 30 miles on a tank of water. Clean, soft water was preferable as scale from hardness in the water was deposited in the tubes and lessened the intervals at which they had to be blown out.

It will have been observed, from what has been written earlier, that boiler feed was catered for by two pumps. The regular water supply was provided by a pump gear driven from the engine and calculated, so long as the lorry was in motion, to provide sufficient water to the steam generator for ordinary requirements. The second pump, known as the 'donkey pump', was fitted on the offside of the chassis below the cab. The pump had one double acting steam cylinder, with mushroom valves, and a double ram water end. The primary purpose of it was the injection of extra water - and hence the generation of extra steam - on hills or whenever extra power was required. The makers said in their sales literature, 'on reaching the foot of a hill, the Donkey is used to assist the gear driven pump and the steam pressure can be raised to any desired extent' but, in practice, it was necessary to turn it on somewhat ahead of the hill so as to have the extra steam available when it came to be required.

The paraffin supply depended upon a single pump, again driven off the engine. As the burners worked on the principle of the blow lamp, with the intensity of flame governed by the pressure in the system, the pump was arranged so as to draw paraffin from the 35 gallon main fuel tank and deliver it into the much smaller pressure receiver, where an optimum working pressure of 50/60 psi was maintained. The pressure had to be raised by hand in a dead vehicle before starting but could usually be kept up overnight in a lorry in regular use. From the pressure receiver it was fed to the burner, regulated by the automatic control already

described. To have sufficient fuel available for maximum demand the pump was sized so as to pump in excess of normal running needs, the excess during ordinary running being returned to the main fuel tank through the pressure relief valve and bypass pipe. The set of the relief valve was controllable by a small hand wheel from the driving position and was the means whereby, within limits, the driver controlled the rate of burning.

The chassis of a Sheppee was constructed of standard steel channel, the wheels, springs, axles and chains being bought in. On all production models the front axle was a Butler double channel axle, with nickel steel stubs and the rear axle a solid nickel steel forging. Ground clearance on the H type was nine inches but this was increased on the Overseas Special to eighteen inches, achieved in part by increasing the rear wheels from 34ins diameter to 41ins diameter and in part by a rearrangement of the running gear so as to bring it above the axle centres.

The catalogue, issued in 1914 to press the sales of the overseas model, was extremely optimistic to say the least, and two of its introductory paragraphs are worth quoting at length:

'We were induced to bring out our Overseas Special because we were convinced that a very great potential existed by a light, speedy and powerful steam driven wagon, using ordinary kerosene or paraffin oil as fuel, and designed *throughout* for work Overseas.

'The response has been immediate, and the enormous and increasing number of enquiries which we continually receive from all parts of Africa, India, Australia, New Zealand, Canada, South America, Roumania, Japan, Turkey, France, Holland, Spain, Belgium, Norway, Cuba, Burma, The Levant and the United States of America, not to mention many other countries, has abundantly proved that the demand is no imaginary one and that it has been, and is still being, neglected by the majority of English Manufacturers'.

Who would realise, on reading such a puff, that the only Overseas Special actually built and sold was the Venezuelan wagon? The onset of the 1914 war and subsequent death of Colonel Sheppee put an end to Sheppee steam lorries, as has already been narrated, but had these two events not occurred, it is unlikely that they would have found a continuing market. At a price of £610.00 for a chassis with flat lorry body, the Sheppee H type was selling at roughly the same price as a Garrett or Foden 5 ton overtype on rubber tyres but with only sixty per cent of the latter's carrying capacity or, in real terms, probably less than half. On the credit side, of course, the unladen weight of 3 tons 4 cwt was about half that of the optimistic 'painter's'

The Venezuelan wagon paraded at York racecourse for the photographer.

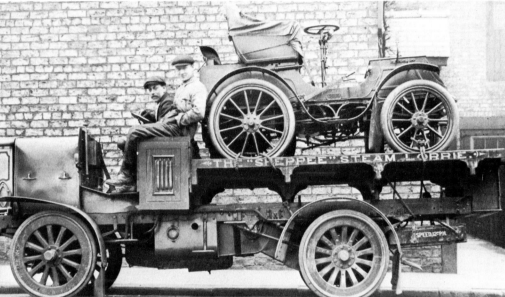

A treasure loaded upon a treasure. What lengths would a collector go to in order to possess either today? About 1911 one of the early wagons brings in a casualty.

Life was not all work in 1911. In this picture the Sheppee staff are returning to York from an outing to Scarborough on one of the works charabancs, registered DN60.

weights of the overtypes. Development of the Sheppee might have produced a wagon as sophisticated as the Doble/Henschels or Doble/Sentinels which, it is argued by their advocates, would have to be the prototypes if the steam vehicle were to become resurgent. This is a debate beyond the scope of this article. In 1914, the Sheppee could make no headway against its cruder but effective steam competitors, a fate which shortly overtook the roughly comparable Clarkson.

*This article cannot be concluded without a note of sincere thanks to those who collaborated with the author in assembling the information - Geoff Stubbington, who first suggested it, and John Meredith, who helped in the initial stages, and a number of members of the Sheppee firm who went to great pains to help. The late Tom Notley has been mentioned in the text, but thanks are extended also to two of the directors, Messrs J L Stabler and A R Bradley, who took a great interest, and the late Mr Len Bell, a director until his premature death, who did so much to further the project.*

# SEEN & HEARD

LEO PRATT TOLD US about this former mobile X Ray unit on a wartime (or is it an early post-war Pax?) Dennis chassis some time ago and if it has not already been rescued, it should hopefully still be found in Arnold's Yard, Stainforth, near Doncaster .....

THIS LATIL 4x4 and four wheel steer timber tractor is available in Norfolk at around £500 (contact Neville Middleton, Litcham 355). It is chassis no 55265 Mk 1 Series A, probably meaning that it is a 1937 London built example following the end of S&D licence assembly in Letchworth that year. Its original Meadows petrol engine has unfortunately (or fortunately, from a practical point of view) been replaced by a P6. It was last used in 1975. On the subject of Latils, Mr Green from Stoke Albany, Market Harborough, tells us that he is still using one of their all British rivals - a 1951 Unipower Hannibal for tree pulling and vehicle recovery. He also uses a Gardner powered Scammell for low-load work

A LOCAL NURSING HOME uses a sparkling thirty year old Bedford ambulance to take its patients to and from Cheltenham Hospital .....

FRIENDS OF THE FIRE SERVICES National Museum Trust are invited to help with the new museum being established at the Home Office Fire Services Technical College, Moreton-in-Marsh, where some early appliances are already housed. Details from the Hon Sec, M G Cole, 9 Morland Way, Manton Heights, Bedford .....

ON A VISIT TO THE 1978 HERSHEY SWAP MEET, Nick Georgano saw these two trucks. The derelict one is easy enough to identify as a 1947 International KB but frankly we were completely foxed by the fire truck until Nick told us that it was another International - a 1944 4x4 .....

THIS 1948 BEDFORD with Vincent body has been derelict on a Hertfordshire farm for some considerable time, despite a speedo reading believed to be genuine of 16,841 miles. Details from A G Delderfield, Wayside, Dudswell, Berkhamsted, who sent us the information ....

CAN ANYONE HELP Peter Serrell (Hartlebury 373) date an Austin Loadstar that he has recently acquired? It is ex-WD and carries chassis number 191949 .....

SEEN IN FRANCE was this forties van with Chenard-Walcker name plate. The design became better known under the Peugeot name after C-W became part of Peugeot in 1951 .....

OUR PHOTO SHOWS A *circa* 1950 Leyland Beaver put out to pasture at Chiltern Queens bus depôt at Woodcote near Reading and apparently in sound order, having been used as a bus recovery truck for many years .....

MIKE MAYO TELLS US of a Fordson WOT1 6x4 truck in a farmyard at Iron Acton, North Avon, three 7Vs near Symonds Yat, the remains of a *c*1929 Thornycroft A1 bus (including chassis, wheels and radiator shell) at Earlswood, Chepstow, a Bedford MWD 15 cwt truck at Mitcheldean and a GPO linesmen's Morris E at Llangwm, Usk .....

OPEN FROM 30TH APRIL to 30th September between 10am and 6pm everyday except Fridays is the new National Tractor and Farm Museum which is just off the A69 Newcastle to Hexham Road, three miles east of Corbridge. It contains the remarkable Moffitt collection of early tractors and a few interesting commercials .....

SEEN ON THE NORTH SIDE of the Firth of Forth was this oil engined Albion of immediately post-war vintage. It was on a farm that abounded in rotting horse-drawn implements .....

THIS HANDSOME TWIN STEER ERF is still in regular service with the makers of Gardner engines. It is still on its original 150 bhp 6LX despite eighteen years on the road .....

AFTER BUILDING 16,000 of their final Big J models since their launch in 1964, the last Guy left the Wolverhampton factory in January 1979. In future, Guy will make their Victory export bus for assembly overseas (where they are called Leylands) and the forthcoming bonneted versions of Leyland's secret (at the time of writing) T45 range. Guy began as a light truck maker in 1914 and had a successful existence until the death of its founder Sydney Guy in 1957. Things then deteriorated fast until, in 1961, it was rescued by Jaguar Cars. As part of the subsequent BMH Group, it would have been their heavy truck division had not the Leyland take-over in 1968 changed this plan and spelt the ultimate end of Guy .....

IF YOU CAN CONVINCE BOC that your truck preservation is an Industrial Preservation Scheme and if you use their gas equipment in its restoration, then they may be willing to give you assistance. Contact BOC Ltd, Peel Road, Skelmersdale, Lancs, for details .....

MARTIN PERRY FROM BROMYARD reports a number of interesting finds, including the Second World War 4x4 Ford V8 shown clearing dead elms near his garage last winter. He says that Sheppard Government Surplus Yard, Upper Hill, Leominster, has the remains of a Proctor lorry (reg EUT 919) and a JNSN that they broke up, but they still have some interesting ex-WD bits and pieces. He also mentions a QL Bedford and some Jeeps in a yard just off the A38 south of Quedgeley .....

A READER IN WORTHING has just acquired a 30 cwt Vulcan rolling chassis via a complex chain of events. A demolition gang on the Isle of Wight found it in a concrete shed and attempted to flatten it with a JCB. Failing that, they loaded it onto a scrap lorry and, on its way to the dump, a passing BRS driver spotted the load and passed on the details to Reo bus owner John Golding. He, in turn, told local enthusiast (and Great War Fiat truck owner) Richard Peskett who, knowing of G L Abbot's liking for Vulcans, passed on its whereabouts to him. The grapevine certainly works in the South! .....

A THREE TON FORDSON Thames V8 of 1952 in use until a year ago is available from Michael Greenhill, Church House Farm, West Chelborough, Evershot, Dorset .....

A 1929 MORRIS-COMMERCIAL one ton chassis with axles and steering gear is available from Robert Moorhouse, Pear Tree Farm, Wintersett, Wakefield .....

VISIBLE TWO MILES out of Northampton on the Coventry road was this early fifties HD55 Albion eight wheeler until early in 1979. In good order, but supported on trestles, and attached to a fuel pump, it was apparently used for replenishing modern Bulwark tankers. What has become of it? An AEC eight wheeler of similar vintage can be seen at Evans Transport, Renwick Road, Barking .....

A *c*1930 LEYLAND petrol engine and an ex-Karrier Dorman unit languish in Arkinstalls' yard, Guilsfield, Welshpool. Our thanks to Mike Jones for the information which may help someone's restoration .....

WHAT APPEARED TO BE a late thirties Latil 4x4 four wheel steer timber tractor was recently seen trundling under the station bridge at Bicester. We couldn't read the operator's name but it appeared to be still in service - does anyone know where it can be inspected? Also on the subject of timber tractors, we recently encountered an immaculate 1951 Unipower at aptly named East Winch .....

THE NEW MANAGING DIRECTOR of BL Heritage Ltd (formerly British Leyland Historic Vehicles) is Peter Mitchell, who was Senior Keeper of Coventry City's collection of locally built vehicles. Let us hope that he can improve the balance of cars and commercials in the Leyland section of the Donington Collection. At present there are few of Leyland's trucks and buses on show because space is too limited and they are too heavy for the floors, but we have heard rumours of new buildings or even a new venue .....

MORE ON THE BRISTOL LORRY shown in *OLD MOTOR* 11:6 *Tea & Wads* from M J Tozer of the Bristol Interest Circle, 65 Westward Drive, Pill, Bristol. He tells us that the vehicle was new in 1925 to Chesterfield Corporation and had a 31 seat Bristol body. It and five sisters were part exchanged for Leylands TD1s in 1931 and some or all of them became trucks. On the subject of the same article, John Bland feels that the Riker shown is either its forerunner, a Locomobile, or else a Pierce-Arrow. He says that the Pierce-Arrow shown has a non-standard radiator. On the same subject still, Maurice Doggett is fairly certain that the Pierce-Arrow, Berna and Leyland Bull all belonged to Union Cartage .....

IN THIS TANTALISING GLIMPSE into a shed in Central France can be seen a very original GMC 6x6 and beside it a Berliet, presumably also of the Second World War years .....

# TRAINS OFF TRACKS

**The idea of emulating the railways and towing great trains of trailers on the road has long appealed to vehicle designers and operators. ARTHUR INGRAM examines what has been achieved since 1900 and points out the practical drawbacks to road trains in many countries.**

THE idea of running road trains similar to those used on the iron roads was something that appealed to freight carriers from the early days of the century. True, there had been ponderous steam tractors with their gangling collection of agricultural implements, water carts and living vans, before that but these were hardly practical locomotives for long distance transport, though some were used with trains of trailers for leisurely household removal.

Credit for the first practical system of a powered road train must go to Colonel Renard of the French Army, who designed such a thing just after the turn of the century. In 1903 the

Société Francaise des Trains Renards was established in Paris and a prototype unit built by the Darracq concern. It was duly exhibited at the Paris Salon, powered by a 4 cylinder 60hp petrol engine.

The Renard design called for a four wheeled powered tractor and two or more trailers, with a crew of three ostensibly - driver, steersman and brakeman. A major design feature was that the trailers were also powered by the engine in the tractor, the drive being taken the length of the train by means of a jointed drive shaft. A flexible joint was provided between tractor and each subsequent trailer, and the drive was thence by a

worm driven countershaft and side chains to the centre pair of wheels on the three axle trailers. The tractor had its rear wheels driven by a worm drive countershaft and side chains. The front wheels of the tractor steered in the normal way and the movement was conveyed to the first trailer by swivelling steering rods running from the rear of the tractor to the leading axle of the first trailer. In order for the trailers to follow the tractor unit precisely, the rear axle of each also steered. As counter lock to that of the leading axle of the trailer was required, it was achieved by connecting the front and rear axle of each trailer by means of crossed

Colonel Renard's system was taken up by Daimler of Coventry and here we see one of their road trains at work in Canada in 1911.

cables. So, as the tractor was steered to the left the steering bar moved the leading axle of the first trailer also to the left, but the crossed cable arrangement ensured that the rear axle of the trailer steered to the right so ensuring 'tracking' in the path established by the tractor unit.

Although rarely used in practice, there was a facility for steering the train in reverse. In this case the brakeman or rear steersman would take hold of a tiller attached to the rear axle of the last trailer and manually swing the trailer in the required direction!

One of the earliest road trains was exported to Persia in 1904 and on this occasion a steam engine was specified, although orders supplied to operators in Belgium and France used a 72hp Turgan Foy built petrol engine.

In 1904 the English Daimler company became interested in the project, no doubt with an eye on the large Colonial potential of the product. Part of the sales pitch used by Renard was that the road train was eminently suitable for cross-

country use by virtue of the fact that every unit in the train was powered. This design feature obviated the risk of bogging down by the leading driven vehicle, for if one drive unit hit a soft patch then, in theory at least, the remainder kept it on the move.

Daimlers negotiated to handle the Renard in all countries outside

France. Their version of the train originally used a four cylinder petrol engine but this was dropped in 1909 in favour of the 9.4 litre six cylinder Daimler-Knight sleeve valve unit.

Each Renard trailer had its centre axle driven from the tractor, whilst its fore and aft axles steered in opposite directions to each other to maintain tracking.

This 1925 road train in America looks far too much for the truck to cope with in snowy conditions, until one notices the front wheel tyre chains and realises that the truck is a 4x4 Oshkosh.

Drive was thence by means of a cone clutch and four speed gearbox.

Two of the Daimler-Renard trains were used for demonstration purposes at the 1909 Franco-British Exhibition of 1909, before going to India. One was fitted out as a mixed freight and passenger train, while the second had open cross-bench type passenger cars seating 30 persons. For freight use the capacity of each trailer was said to be 5 tons.

The speed of the road train was around 10 mph maximum, while the gradient ability was stated to be as good as 1 in 5.

A handsome triple unit in America hauled by a 1931 White 641 and used for taking bottled milk to distribution centres where each trailer could be left for unloading.

This is the original 1931 petrol engined AEC tractor. Like the Leyland which followed it into production, it steered on its front and rear axles and drove on all eight wheels. Though for only 6 tons each, the Dyson trailers used 8 tyres to minimise ground pressure.

Although the road train was advertised until 1913 it did not attract many buyers. There are reports of trains being shipped to Australia, Canada, USA, South America, Burma and Uruguay, and a shortened version was used by the Daimler concern themselves for inter-works transport. Quantity orders do not seem to have been forthcoming except for the two that went to India and in Australia where 'several' were thought to have been in use. So far as is known, none have survived.

Whether the early demise of the Renard system was as a result of high cost, slow speed, weight, undue wear or whatever is not obvious, although

it could be that the intervention of the First World War and the great strides made in heavy vehicles during the twenties made a lorry and trailer arrangement more practical.

Although road vehicles had proved their superiority during the 1914-18 war, the military authorities were naturally anxious to improve things further - particularly the cross country movement of supplies. After the success of the Foster tank it was natural that tracked vehicles should come under close scrutiny, together with those employing all-wheel drive, widely articulating bogies and the use of temporary tracks around large section pneumatic tyres. Much valuable work was done in the late 1920s by many vehicle builders, including Thornycroft, Guy, FWD and Scammell in Britain, and then in the early 1930s the Overseas Mechanical Transport Directing Committee, which had been set up by the Colonial Office Conference of 1927 to study and report on the possibilities of improving transport in the colonies. They announced that experiments with a heavy tractor unit for towing a series of trailers across open country were at an advanced stage. In 1932 brief details were released of the vehicle - it was to be on the road train principle with an eight wheeled tractor unit and two eight wheel trailers. The tractor unit was to be powered and steered on all four axles and the trailers were to be carried on independent bogies for

A pair of Leyland Super Hippos with 200 bhp 0.680 diesels at work in Australia some twenty years ago, though outwardly similar trucks are still produced today by Leyland for rugged overseas operation.

maximum flexibility. Should the experimental petrol engined version be successful, then a diesel engined edition would soon follow.

In due course, the outfit was presented to the Military at the 1932 Aldershot Tattoo. It consisted of an eight wheeled Leyland tractor unit, which itself could carry a small load, powered by a petrol engine and tow two eight wheeled Dyson trailers for loads of 6 tons each. After its appearance at Aldershot, the road train was shipped out to the Gold Coast for further evaluation and worked the 240 miles between Kumasi and Tamale.

A modern day road train in Australia consisting of a 226 bhp AEC Mammoth Major and three trailers with an all-up weight of more than 50 tons.

It was decided that further units should be oil engined and so in 1933 AEC were asked to construct a road train tractor somewhat similar to the Leyland unit but with their, by then, familiar 6 cylinder 130hp diesel engine.

The eight wheeled tractor unit was of all wheel drive layout with the first and fourth axles steering. The engine was mounted high up at the front of the chassis between the two front seats. The drive was taken through a large diameter dry single plate clutch to the main four speed and reverse gearbox mounted behind the cab, thence through a three speed auxiliary gearbox to a train of gears on the rear axle and then by jointed shafts to the forward three axles. Each of the four axles had its own differential and they were not lockable. A large

cooling radiator was mounted at the back of the cab, well out of the way of any long grass through which the vehicle might travel.

As with the previous unit, the tractor was rated for a payload of 3 tons and the two Dyson double bogie trailers at 6 tons each providing a total load capacity of 15 tons. The tractor used modified AEC 'Marshal' bogies, and the trailer bogies were carried on turntables with connections between them to ensure tracking of the trailers behind the tractor unit.

With a top speed of around 28 mph and a laden gradient ability

**Double bottom outfits have not been seen in Britain, although in the sixties York Trailers brought in this Kenworth/York outfit to demonstrate its feasibility on British roads to the Ministry of Transport.**

of 1 in 6.5, the whole outfit measured 71ft 8ins in length and required a 58ft turning circle.

Examples of the AEC/Dyson road train were shipped to Africa, Russia and Australia and one was in use in the Australian Outback until the 1950s and was languishing in the bush as recently as ten years ago.

Recent types of road train have been for paved roads and have tended to follow a more orthodox layout with a powerful tractor unit towing several trailers. In Australia, in particular, the scene has been dominated by Foden, Mack, Kenworth and Atkinson outfits consisting of perhaps an eight wheel rigid towing two or three trailers. Another variation is the articulated vehicle towing one or two trailers. Naturally these vehicles require plenty of room

to manoeuvre and their use is limited to the less populated areas of the country.

Another country which allows long trains in certain locations is the United States. The 'double bottom' outfit consisting of an articulated vehicle towing another trailer has been in use in certain states since the 1920s, while the longer 'treble', consisting of an artic plus two trailers, has seen somewhat less use for obvious reasons. One interesting variation on this theme was tried several years ago, this consisting of a powered bogie under one of the trailers which could be brought into use as required by the driver for additional power to surmount hills. Another ingenious scheme in America around 1960 was the Wolf Wagon. This consisted of a train of self contained trucks that could be driven from the forward cab as one unit or divided into separate collection and delivery vehicles. Perhaps this scheme will be revived one day. It would make the best use of expensive fuel and drivers' wages and would allow great trains to work the world's trunk routes with several engines cut out yet able to run when the train was divided outside cities on the route. On second thoughts, just think of the union problems that would create!

**A mid-sixties AEC Majestic road train in Australia with prominent 'roo bar on the front to protect radiator and screen. An even more spectacular outfit was one hauled by a Scammell Contractor converted to a rigid eight.**

# TRYING A TILLER

Ancient vehicles take a lot of getting used to, but as NICK BALDWIN recently found out,
the S&D Freighter was such an unusual concept that it would not
be outclassed even today in congested urban collection or delivery,
thanks to its foolproof tiller controls.

IT is all too easy when driving and then writing about an old vehicle to go in for jokey old time English and to heap ridicule on the unfortunate machine because it is not as capable as today's products. Vintage truck road tests nowadays seem to be confined to Christmas issues and a carnival atmosphere that contrasts absurdly with the down-to-earth character of the subjects. What, after all, could be more basic than a dustcart (true, not today's sophisticated refuse collectors) and driving a fifty-year-old example should not be an occasion for dressing up in music hall clothes and devising party tricks for it to perform.

Now, having set what I hope is a suitably responsible and serious tone, for the fun! And fun it was to drive the oldest S&D in existence, though I doubt whether its original drivers would have necessarily agreed with me. The extraordinary thing about it was its practical design and operation. Other old trucks I

have driven could plainly do a good day's work but would be hopelessly outclassed by today's standards of speed and economy. Not so the S&D. Admittedly, with only 20 mph available it would be slow to reach its refuse dump (which didn't matter in days when dumps were close to towns) and its body would not hold enough of today's lightweight bulky refuse, but apart from that it showed a number of features in advance of all but today's automatic transmission vehicles.

The S&D must have been revolutionary when it appeared in 1922. It was the first of the small wheeled freighters, and its easy access and loading, its manoeuvrability and its semi automatic transmission (epicyclic on the same principle as the contemporary Ford Model T) must have been widely appreciated by operators and drivers more used to horses.

Although its transversely mounted 15.8 RAC hp four cylinder monobloc

Jack Hubbard, S&D's chief demonstration driver for some forty years, explains the controls to Nick Baldwin. He promises that the nasty rally plaques will be removed forthwith, by the way.

Out on the road, Jack drives while Nick looks on from a draughty vantage point to learn the technique.

engine drives the rear wheels in the conventional way, the controls are anything but conventional and I was a little apprehensive when Jack Hubbard, chief demonstration driver from 1936 until his recent retirement, explained them to me. Virtually everything required is operated by the two tillers on either side of the driver. On the floor is simply an accelerator, a gong and a brake pedal working front wheel brakes, which are seldom required as the left hand tiller has a brake position operating on the transmission. When moving the tiller from brake one passes either clockwise or anti-clockwise through a

neutral position in which the vehicle is still automatically braked. Carry on clockwise and you encounter first gear which engages smoothly as the first of four separate dry plate clutches in the transmission system bites home. Meanwhile, you have been accelerating away and as speed picks up, you move the tiller on to second and then third, the tiller automatically making allowances in the engine speed. To slow down and brake you simply do the opposite. On the other side of the brake position the same thing happens in reverse, but though contemporary literature speaks of three reverse gears, I could only find two - perhaps explained by the changed specification of S&D's own vehicle which began life in 1927 but was returned to 1922 spec when it was restored by the apprentices in 1968.

On the right, the tiller steering, which is very light with several turns lock to lock, takes even less getting used to than the gears. In fact, the only difficulty I experienced was in moving the gear tiller smoothly, but Jack Hubbard assured me that if one

anchored one's elbow on the side of the seat and used the finer control of one's wrist and forearm, this was soon overcome. Naturally, the driving position is rather exposed without windows or doors and one is thankful for the nice warm radiator in easy reach of one's left hand. Ignition advance is automatic and apart from an oil pressure plunger and an eye on the road, there is nothing else to concern the driver. Even lubrication is automatic, providing you top up the engine and gearbox, and there are no greasers. Starting is by handle, which can be inserted at either the engine or transmission side to ensure that you never get immobilised in a tight alleyway. Though the handle is rather low for hand cranking it is ideal for kick starting!

On the road the S&D is just what you would expect - rather bouncy and pitchy unladen with excellent acceleration, but a painfully slow top speed made up for in urban driving by very good manoeuvrability, thanks to a turning circle of 21 feet. Jack Hubbard told me that on pre-

war demonstrations it was the getting between the factory and one's destination that was tedious. It once took him 3 days to do a Scottish trip, and a journey from Newcastle-on-Tyne to the factory at Letchworth took from 4am to 4pm going flat out and coasting wherever this increased his speed. Orders were not hard to come by because the loading foremen were usually encouraged to give their opinions and S&D were happy to build in any features they

**Gaining a bit of experience as a bin man riding in the only place available for a passenger. In practice, the loaders walked from street to street until on later models a row of seats was built in behind the driver.**

**What it is like looking towards the rear of the vehicle with the seat and 'bonnet' removed. The engine drives across the chassis to an epicyclic gearbox on the other side of the seat and thence to a worm back axle.**

**Tailpiece to an interesting driving experience. The tail gate is unlocked from a lever at the front and only then can the body be tipped. Though the rear wheels have brake drums they do not contain anything but are simply there to be interchangeable with the front wheels. All photos by courtesy of Malcolm Bates of Shelvoke and Drewry Ltd.**

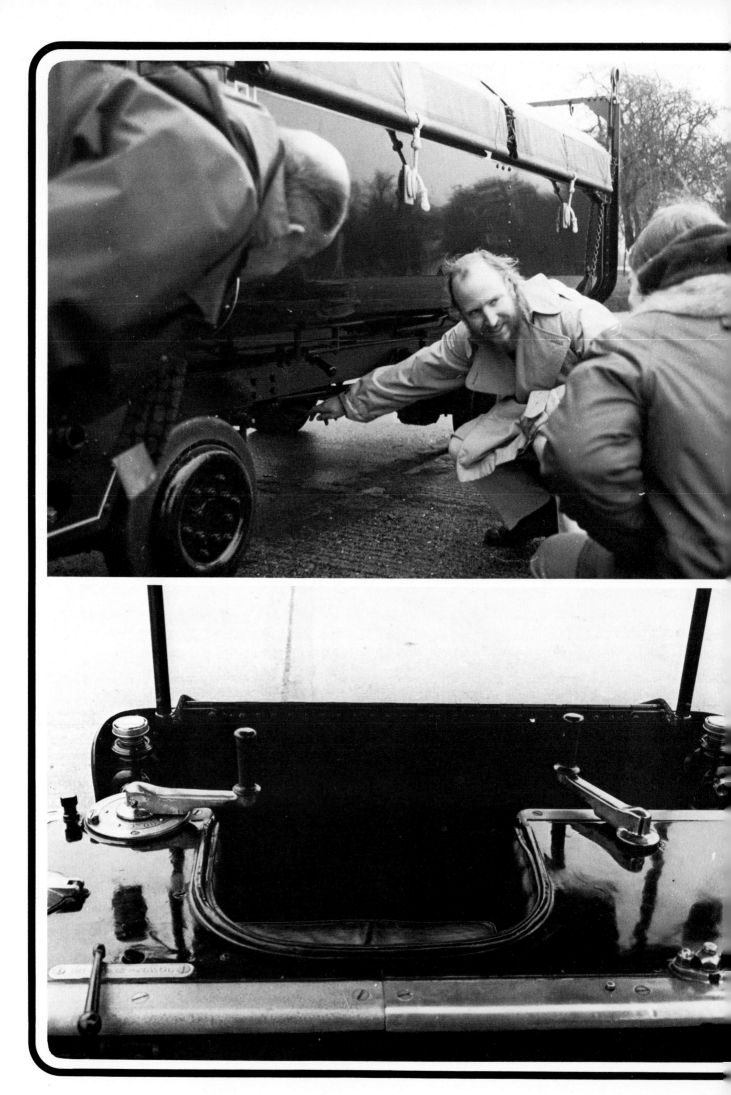

requested. Each vehicle had a 3 year guarantee and in the case of some particularly awkward customers this was sometimes known to be extended to no less than ten years. Jack Hubbard said he had seen loading teams send their S&D off down the street without a driver by leaving it at idling speed in first gear with its wheels against the kerb. They could then line up the dustbins ahead of it and load the S&D as it went by!

For so early a vehicle, it is rather surprising to find that the nine cubic yard steel body with its canvas and teak top is hydraulically tipped - not hand hydraulically, either, but mechanically from a pump integral with the gearbox. The loading rail is only five feet off the ground and payload is about two tons.

This particular S&D started life as a demonstrator in June 1927 when it cost £688-10-0d and two years later it was sold to the Borough of Folkestone. They used it for refuse collection until 1946 at an average stop-start mileage of about 5000 a year. In addition, during the war, it acted as a Civil Defence lorry by night. Afterwards it was used as a sewer maintenance vehicle until February 1966 when it was pensioned off due to its differential failing because of lack of oil.

Though the Freighter was conceived by Mr Shelvoke and Mr Drewry, when they worked at Lacre Lorries, as an ingenious and economical (10-15 mpg) alternative to normal trucks, it is hardly surprising that it was to municipalities that it appealed in particular. Nevertheless, hundreds were sold for less specialised transport duties in the twenties and thirties and the same mechanical arrangements and tiller steerings were kept on all but the smallest S&Ds until the early fifties. A forthcoming book in our *Kaleidoscope* series will show some 200 examples of the amazingly varied types of vehicle made by S&D and the often bizarre uses they were put to. At the same time, we will be showing how the design was conceived and how it worked, though in the meantime I should perhaps attempt to explain to the more technically minded how the unique transmission works.

The gears are in constant mesh and on each end of the main gearbox shaft are dry plate clutches. When the one nearest the radiator is engaged it locks in bottom gear and when the one nearest the engine is engaged you have second. When both are clutched, direct drive top gear operates. Another shaft runs at right angles to the main shaft by means of bevel gearing and it has two further clutches which, because they are on different sides of the bevel, operate in different directions. When one is engaged the vehicle goes forward and when the other is, it goes backward. As they are rotating in opposite directions, it is simply a matter of partly engaging both simultaneously to give braking and this is done automatically by the tiller, which also drops the engine revs to idling when the tiller is moved and then corrects the revs to the road speed on engagement of the next gear.

As you can see, absurdly simple yet extremely effective and a major contribution to what must be one of the most superbly functional vehicles ever designed, and certainly one of the most pleasant to drive - in good weather!

# CABS "OFF THE PEG"

**Have you ever wondered why so many trucks made since the war
bear a striking similarity to each other?
Well the answer in many cases is Motor Panels and their cleverly conceived
universal cabs, from which has also grown
an important sideline in bespoke cabs for several of today's major truck makers.**

THERE are thousands of unsung firms behind the scenes in the motor industry making components for the big car and truck manufacturers to assemble. Individual component firms may supply just one small pressing or fabrication or perhaps a simple washer or split pin, yet all share an important rôle with the big

boys like Automotive Products, Girling Lucas and Pressed Steel, whose products are household names.

Amongst these myriad component suppliers is one very unusual firm whose name is little known outside the industry and yet whose products not only shape the face of many of

today's trucks but are designed to meet legal and production requirements in countries all around the world. The firm is Motor Panels

**A 1952 Thornycroft Trident with the original type of Owen/Motor Panels standard cab. The Trident had Thornycroft's own 6 cylinder 78 bhp diesel and was a 6/7 tonner.**

The other regular user of the standard Mk 1 cab was Guy, and here we see one of the last examples of 1958 before Guy switched temporarily to their own fibreglass design.

(Coventry) Ltd and their principal product is truck cabs.

Motor Panels started in 1924 as one of the little behind-the-scenes firms making car bodywork. They were not bodybuilders so much as panel suppliers to motor factories. In the early days most of these panels were, of course, hand beaten, though Motor Panels specialised in press-work and at times before the war 160 and more panel beaters were on their payroll. Chief memory of old time employees is the deafening noise that they made, though today this is almost forgotten, with only 6 panel beaters left (mainly for one-off proto-type work) and all the rest in the capable jaws of vast mechanical presses. Much of their pre-war work was for SS Jaguar (who, for a time actually owned the firm) and this work carried on afterwards for the

Apparently a prototype of how the Mk 1 cab might have been adapted for use by Thorny-croft. Interestingly enough, a pencilled note on the back of the photo refers to TVW, who may also have considered this style when they acquired the remnants of Sentinel.

The original cab style was also used in small numbers by Kew Dodge, British Mack and AEC. This Dodge was the most familiar on the rare occasions that an operator required a forward control version.

This three ton capacity diesel engined Heron of 1955 had Dennis' own cab but the roof panel was a standard pressing from Motor Panels.

AEC sent out their chassis to specialist cab builders in the early fifties and whether this Motor Panels cab was fitted by one of these firms or whether AEC was considering fitting the Motor Panels cab themselves is lost in the mists of time.

new Bristol car, the Armstrong-Siddeley Sapphire, the Triumph Renown, then the Vanguard estate and van side panels and various Alvis models (including, later, the 6x6 military vehicles). Later came the Jensen, Interceptor and FF and the Jensen-Healey, as well as the lengthened body for the Daimler limousine at the rate of 6-12 each week and for the world's most expensive car, the Rolls-Royce Camargue - 'a very difficult job technically', I was told by Bob Allen, the technical director, 'because of its enormous expanses of almost flat panelling which can show every imperfection'.

All these car body panels are pressed but also require specialist hand finishing which is accomplished by 360 sheet metal works at an associate company.

In 1943 Sir Alfred Owen took over Motor Panels and it joined his Rubery Owen group, perhaps best known then, as now, for its chassis manufacture. After the war, Sir Alfred decided that demand from the car firms for panels was too fluctuating and that the firm should try and break into the truck market, where export was of vital importance and where the traditional coachbuilt cab methods had fallen twenty years behind car bodies. Traditional metal clad wooden frames were often unacceptable overseas and whilst such firms as Leyland could afford to tool up for all steel Comet cabs there were few other firms large enough to stand the expenditure.

Motor Panels conceived a 'Universal' cab to solve the problem for these smaller makers. It employed standardised pressings to keep the cost down (even the left and right hand doors were interchangeable) and could have individual frontal styling features or space for a traditional radiator.

As well as their standard cabs, Motor Panels continued to make specific parts for the large volume van makers. They made the side panels for the original and later van and estate car versions of the Vanguard.

Motor Panels turned both the Minx and the Super Snipe into pick-ups for the Rootes Group. This is the so-called Commer Light Pick-up.

For all the soundness of the idea, Motor Panels found themselves up against endless problems. They took the cab round the truck makers and soon had to drop the term 'Universal' when they saw some of the things that it was expected to fit! Many truck firms were extremely sceptical about the project and most said that there was no point fitting it to existing chassis with new models in the pipeline, and yet would not take the cab makers into their confidence to show them the 'secret' models. In the end, only Thornycroft and Guy bought the cab in any numbers, hence the outward similarity between these two firms' medium weight trucks in the early fifties. Thornycroft added to MP's problems by insisting on a cab divided at the waist for the Sturdy Star and Trident so that they could ship chassis/cabs 'knocked down' to the tops of their steering columns. They also asked for, and got, a widened shell for use on the Antar tank transporter, which in those early years was using the Rover Meteorite engine.

Dennis compromised by making their own cabs fitted with the roof panel from the ex-Universal cab (now called the Mark 1) and both Kew Dodge and the British Mack set-up at Barking bought a few Motor Panels cabs for special purposes and at any rate one AEC Mandator was photographed with the cab.

Whilst endeavouring to sell the Mark 1 cab, Motor Panels were also involved with lesser panelwork for various commercial vehicles, including doors, roof panels and front for the boxy Morris-Commercial one ton van, pick-up bodies for the Commer derivative of the Hillman Minx and bodies for export pick-up versions of the rugged Super Snipe, much used in the oil-fields before the virtues of the Land-Rover became widely known. By the late fifties the Mark 1 cab's styling and interior design were becoming dated and Dodge asked Motor Panels to produce a special cab to

This was a proposed facelift for the LAD cab that was prepared for Albion. A number of other ideas were tried, but in the end Sankey's Ergomatic cab was used on Albions not supplied with the basic LAD design to save tooling costs.

The second generation of standard cab was the one adopted by Seddon in 1964 and called their Supa cab.

their requirements. Leyland were also on the lookout for a new cab (and were using Motor Panels for the supply of Albion Claymore panels) and after consultations with Dodge, the two firms agreed to share the development costs and own a proportion of the complex tooling jointly. This was born the famous LAD cab (Leyland-Albion-Dodge) which, though replaced by Dodge in the mid-sixties, continued to serve Albion for another ten years. Indeed, the last, admittedly only for spares stock, was not delivered until early in 1979, after some 135,000 similar cabs had been sold. Whilst all these LAD cabs were basically similar, the front panel was, of course, individual to each manufacturer and there were other differences, like the longer doors on Albions - a modification that Dodge looked at with a certain amount of envy. Incidentally, when the LAD was first planned, Triplex did not believe that such an expanse of single pane windscreen was possible - how times change, it looks

This is the Mk III cab as exemplified by Foden's S40. The Mk III was a widened version of the Mk II and Foden were the first to use it on vehicles for the British market.

Werklust are a Dutch construction machinery firm who introduced this ingenious front wheel drive 6x2 skip carrier that required no lifting arms. The cab was a Mk III with extra rear windows.

An interesting mock-up produced for the specialist Dutch truck manufacturer Terberg around 1970 used the basic Mk II structure with an identical cab roof pressing doing duty as bonnet top. Instead, Terberg used Mercedes, and then Volvo cabs to satisfy their very small output.

downright pokey now! From 1966 Dodge used a new angular cab exclusively for their 500 series and this was styled by an American working at Kew and engineered by Motor Panels for assembly at Coventry, though at the last minute Dodge found they had the capacity to assemble it themselves.

Meanwhile, the standard cab as used by Thornycroft and Guy (until replaced by fibreglass in 1958) had been superseded by a second generation version, which was adopted by Seddon for their new 13:Four and Guy for their Big J range, both announced in 1964. A wide version

Guy were the other original users of the second generation cab on their Big J range and here we see an early 1967 version in slightly unfamiliar form with a sleeping compartment [also made by MP].

of this Mk II cab was available from 1967/8 but was adopted by only Foden for home consumption, though ERF used it on some export models, including their famed Jordanian phosphate truck contract. Overseas it was bought by Bernard, or rather by Mack, who then owned this respected old French manufacturer. Mack soon withdrew from their French involvement and much of the technical work was transferred to Floors, the Mack distributors in Holland, who soon adopted the Motor Panels cab for their FTF trucks.

Next came the Mark III cab used by Guy and Seddon again and by ERF, Scammell, Crusader, RABA of Hungary (whose prototypes were exhaustively tested at MIRA - the first foreigners to be allowed on this secret proving ground), Shelvoke and Drewry, Mack, Floor, Vickers (who became known as Crane Travellers and then Jones, who still use MP cabs), Argyle Werklust (who make an ingenious front wheel drive 6x2 skip carrier), Unipower for their new Invader and Foden (who called

The Scammell Crusader uses a Mk III cab with fibreglass front panels [which show up here against the white painted steel]. This is an early Detroit engined version.

Various attempts were made to give Atkinson a steel cab and a few were built with MP cabs and traditional radiators. Shown here is an aesthetically more pleasing mock-up of a Mk III complete with giant emblem from an Omega desert tractor.

it their S40 cab). Latest in the line is the Mk IV used by most of the previous customers (in Foden's case it is their S90), plus the newcomer of 1977, Dennison in Eire, and S&D with their new non-municipal SPV range.

A feature of Commercial Motor Shows since the fifties has been Motor Panels' display of a trend-setting cab for the future. These incorporate features which are always carefully examined by operators and truck makers who produce their own cabs. In 1957 it was very high cabs that were seen to be coming and later sleeper cabs (you'll never seen one of those in Britain, said one well-known truck manufacturer) and the use of aluminium (so far only to be found in service on the other side of the Atlantic).

Nowadays, Motor Panels make their standard cabs as well as 'private' ones for particular makers. They also design, style, tool (including making the special tools and dies) for customers who plan actual assembly overseas. In this way, the Czechoslovakian LIAZ trucks were

An unusual derivation of the Mk III cab is used by Jones on their Crane Traveller chassis. This is its forerunner when made by Vickers All Wheel Drive at Swindon. A similar cab with centre steering is used on Scammell's new crash tenders.

This was to have been the MP equipped new French Mack following the purchase of Bernard by the American company. However, following the collapse of Bernard the rights passed to Floor in Holland.

An example of Floor's FTF heavy tractor which is the standard Dutch Army tank transporter. Floor have used various generations of MP cab going back to the Mk II, though this is the wider Mk III.

Much of the background engineering, including cab work for Hungary's RABA, took place in Britain and here an early example is seen on the pavé at the Motor Industry Research Association track in the Midlands.

ERF have long been keen advocates of plastics cabs but have often fitted Motor Panels steel structures to export chassis, notably the fifty Rolls-Royce engineered 6x4 tractors for 50 tons gtw supplied to Jordan in 1968.

tooled way back in 1969/70 but only seen in the West for the first time some six years later.

Motor Panels came close to making a British cab for the Scottish assembled Volvos, but are kept busy instead on setting up an assembly line for an exciting new range of trucks to be announced shortly, which will incorporate the most up-to-date cab and general engineering technology in Europe. Two other current special jobs are the cabs for the Seddon-Atkinson 200, 300 and 400 series and the space frames for ERF to bolt their special plastic panels to for the widely acclaimed B and M series trucks.

Current cab production is running at 48,000 per year and this will soon climb to 80,000 as more and more truck manufacturers decide to leave cab production to the specialists in much the way that they do at present with axles, wheels, frames, propshafts, brakes and often even engines and transmissions. At the 1978

Motor Show a prototype modular MP5 narrow cab was shown as a trend for the future - on past form it should become a production reality early in the eighties.

A variation on the Motor Panels Mk III theme was this early European specification ERF unit with its distinctive frontal styling.

The cabs for Seddon-Atkinson's 200, 300 and 400 series [an example of the latter shown with Cummins 328 bhp six cylinder diesel] styled by Seddon and engineered, tooled and assembled by Motor Panels with final trimming by the chassis maker.

Another example of a special cab designed by the customer in conjunction with MP is the ERF B series, new in 1974. The steel underframe is made by MP and ERF then bolt hot press moulded plastics panels to it.

Shelvoke & Drewry used the Motor Panels cab on their N series municipal chassis of 1972 to 1978 and now use the Mk IV cab [best known on Foden's Haulmaster and Fleetmaster] on their new SPV purpose-built vehicles.

# The W&G Legend

**In what is surely one of the most extraordinary tales from the early motor industry, TED GAFFNEY looks at the amazing multi-million pound background to Willy and George's make of commercial vehicles and tries to discover what went wrong.**

THE six du Cros sons and their father, William Harvey du Cros, played a major rôle in the birth of the motor industry which is all but forgotten today.

Pronounced *dewcrow*, the family were Huguenots who had escaped French religious persecution in 1704 and settled in Ireland. There they fought in the British Army and showed no signs of an industrial bent

before the birth of William Harvey on 19th June 1846. By all accounts he had an unhappy childhood and left home at the age of 15 to fend for himself. He was only 5ft 5ins tall, tough and wiry, with a typical Irish charm. After taking any jobs he could get, he settled as a bookkeeper in Dublin where, by the age of 22, he was earning the modest sum of £90 per annum and had a wife and two

sons to support. A year later he climbed the first rung of success when he became assistant secretary of the Irish Commercial Travellers Association, a sedentary job which led his doctor to advise him to take

**The first of 500 Panhard taxis put on London's streets by W & G in 1909. The vehicle had a monobloc four cylinder 12/15hp engine and the du Cros family were, of course, concessionaires for the make.**

Some of the du Cros brothers on their 'ordinaries' in the 1880s.

William Harvey du Cros, founder of the Dunlop Pneumatic Tyre Co, and a major force in the early motor industry both in France and England.

up sport. With typical thoroughness, and at the age of thirty, he became a first rate athlete, an impressive Rugby player who became captain of the Irish team, a champion boxer and fencer and, perhaps most important of all, a keen cyclist.

By now he had six sons, Harvey Junior, Alfred, Arthur, Frederick, George and William, and these he encouraged to take up manly sporting pursuits. Several became leading cyclists and Arthur ultimately world champion.

By the 1880s father du Cros had become president of the Irish Cyclists Association and a well known Dublin figure. One day in 1888 he was approached by William Bowden, a Dublin bicycle shop owner, and his newspaper publishing friend, J M Gillies, to see if he would be interest in helping them to promote the patents that they had just acquired from Belfast vet J B Dunlop for a pneumatic bicycle tyre. The advantages of the tyre were by no means clear cut as in 1889 W Hume beat all comers riding a pneumatic tyre equipped safety bicycle, only to be trounced a few

weeks later by Arthur on solid tyres in the 5 Mile All Ireland Championship. Despite this, the boys agreed that the new tyres improved comfort and, before long, speed as well. Indeed, when Arthur, as Irish champion, turned up at a race at Kennington Oval in 1890, he was promptly banned because of the 'unfair advantage' of his pneumatic tyres. On the strength of his sons' findings, Harvey Senior decided to promote the Dunlop tyre on the understanding that he should have

complete control and appoint the directors. Thus was born the Pneumatic Tyre and Booth's Cycle Agency Ltd which, in 1896, with the move from Dublin to Coventry to be nearer the cycle market and industry, became the Dunlop Pneumatic Tyre Co, in which the major shareholder outside the du Cros family was none other than their old family friend, Adolphe Clément, the French cycle and then car manufacturer. Harvey Senior was the only executive director of the original firm, until joined by son Arthur as joint managing director, and whilst vast fortunes were made by almost everyone concerned with the firm, it is interesting to note that J B Dunlop sold his shareholding before the formation of the new company and made, at most, £100,000. He could not believe that there was a future for pneumatic tyres outside the bicycle industry and when the earlier Thompson patents were discovered and the du Cros firm no longer had a monopoly, he thought he saw the writing on the wall. Much later he tried to stop the use of his familiar portrait as the Dunlop trademark, claiming it to be an unfair caricature amongst other things. He failed!

All the du Cros sons were roped in to help with the tyre and were sent to the four corners of the world to grab all sales opportunities. By a stroke of good fortune, Harvey Senior was able to buy the Welch patents for

detachable tyres with wired-on beads (the rights cost £5000 for Britain and Belgium and £2500 for France and North America) and thus keep the technical lead required following the loss of the monopoly.

The bicycle firms were reluctant to see their narrow-section solid tyres disappear, but were compelled to adopt the Dunlop tyre by public demand. They believed it to be a nine days wonder, which indeed it might have been if rights to its use had been exclusive to a few firms, including Humber, as the four leading cycle makers wanted.

With the coming of motor vehicles, the pneumatic tyre was, of course, soon adopted for their use and when S F Edge, a former Dunlop departmental manager, won the Gordon Bennett Race in 1902 with an all British Napier-Dunlop combination, the du Cros firm's rather slow transition from bicycle tyres was at last exonerated.

The sons all became deeply embroiled in motoring and now lived in London whilst their father settled at Howberry Park near Wallingford, having sold his first English home, the 5000 acre Cornbury Estate in Oxfordshire in 1901 to Vivian Watney for £110,000.

George accompanied Charles Jarrott as riding mechanic in the 1902 Paris-Vienna Race and described it afterwards as 'better than steeplechasing'! With his brother William, he was joint managing director of the Panhard-Levassor agency, a make for which their father had secured exclusive British and Colonial rights, and a make which he and most of his sons drove. Their friend Adolphe Clément was a director and then chairman of Panhard, as well as of the Clément bicycle and then car firm. In 1896, William Harvey du Cros, with a syndicate of British financiers, had acquired Humber's French factory along with the Clément manufacturing name and some of its production facilities - all a useful captive market for Dunlop's French subsidiary, in which Adolphe Clément had a close interest. At the same time, Harvey Senior and his friends (including Harry Lawson and Ernest Hooley) acquired the A Darracq founded Gladiator concern (whose cars du Cros also sold in Britain, accounting for up to 4/5th of their total 1000+ annual output). Their fellow director in Clément et Gladiator, along with Adolphe Clément, was none other than Alexandre Darracq who, in 1897, left to start the car firm bearing his own name. Clément et Gladiator was run on Harvey

du Cros' behalf by Frank Fenton and its cars were made in Britain for a time from 1907 by another du Cros interest, the Swift Motor Co Ltd. In 1909 Clément et Gladiator was acquired by Vinot et Deguingand, which also had links with du Cros - and Frank Fenton on its board.

With all this talk of motor firm investments, it is interesting to note that the du Cros family also became the largest shareholders in the new Austin Motor Company.

Meanwhile, Harvey Junior was managing director of both the du Cros controlled Swift and Ariel enterprises and, like his brothers, an enthusiastic motorist. As early as 1899 he had entered a partnership with S F Edge and Montague Napier, to become sole agent for the new Napier cars, first conceived when a Napier engine was installed in Edge's four year old Panhard.

In 1903 the Napier factory in Vine Street, Lambeth, had been vacated in favour of a new one at Acton and

there the firm produced big six cylinder luxury cars of 40/60hp. These found a market worldwide, thanks to the energy of S F Edge and the high standard of Napier engineering. The clientele for these expensive cars declined though, particularly as Rolls-Royce, who had been producing twin cylinder cars, moved into this field with their new six cylinder 40/50 model, which was in fact a little cheaper than the Napier in 1907. Napier then concentrated on 4 cylinder cars and went on to produce great numbers of 15hp taxi cabs. Up to that time, London taxicabs were permitted to carry only two persons. This singularly light load necessitated only lightly built bodywork so that a twin cylinder engine was considered an ample power unit, but with motor cabs becoming popular on account of their speed, users were becoming critical of this inadequate capacity, especially as most parties wishing to travel to railway stations comprised more than two people, which meant hiring extra cabs.

It was in 1907 that this anomaly was highlighted, when a cab driver was caught in Whitehall with an excess load, two passengers being seated on the floor of the vehicle. This became a test case, the result of which caused questions to the Home Secretary in the House of Commons about the matter. Later in the autumn of that year, Sir Edward Henry, the Metropolitan Police Commissioner, announced new regulations which had been under review and were to come into force in 1908. These were for motor omnibuses (stage carriages), also the subject of public complaints at that time. These were to be reduced in weight while taxicabs (motor hackneys) were now to be more robustly constructed to carry four persons, two to be accommodated on folding cricket seats behind the driver's partition, facing rearwards. Motor cabs would also require a four cylinder engine to cope with the extra passengers and their luggage, and be fitted with the new taxi meter to avoid arguments over fares between passengers and drivers, which had become too frequent.

Up to this time, London taxicabs were mainly of French make, Renault, Charron and Unic, with British made Wolseley Siddeleys in a minority. The new Napier cabs were substantially built with 4 cylinder engines and complying with the new regulations in all respects and, of course, seating four persons.

On 14th July 1908 W & G du Cros Ltd was formed as a private company, with brothers William and George at the head and sufficient finance from Harvey Senior to put 500 cabs on the road. The W & G headquarters were quite near to

Some of W & G's line-up of Napier vans in 1913, conceived by the crippling strike of taxi drivers.

those of Napier, just oppose *The King's Arms* in Acton Vale. At this time much of Acton was still fields and farms. Just across the Vale from *The King's Arms*, near to Stanley Gardens, a rough track led down to Essex Park Farm. The farmer, Samuel Beech, was one of a number in the Acton district to be ousted by the rapid advance of the new industries which were setting up there. His name and that of his farm live on in the nearby Beech Avenue and Essex Park Mews. Beyond the farm was Acton Council's sewage works where the road petered out and became a public footpath leading to Turnham Green. Bronnley's soap works were already established there and around 1905 C A Vandervell had set up to manufacture dynamo lighting sets. The new W & G premises had a frontage on this track, which was afterwards paved with cobblestones and named Warple Way. Here were the main vehicle entrance and the offices, above which a large electric clock was suspended with the letters 'W & G du Cros Ltd' on the dial instead of the usual numerals.

The garage extended down to where Valetta Road now joins Warple Way. Workshops, engine fitting and body building, stores for the maintenance of a large fleet were disposed over the site, bounded on the east side by Larden Road, with a service road emerging into The Vale which Acton District Council officially named du Cros Road. Early in 1909 construction of the new premises was well in hand and a large order to Napier brought supplies of chassis for cabs.

It was in this same year, following a warning from Lord Roberts, the recently retired commander in chief of the Army, that a German invasion was a possibility. Wyndhams Theatre staged a play entitled *Englishman's Home* which portrayed such an event. For some years, the Army Council had shown interest in mechanical transport, but now an exercise was about to take place in which a battalion was to be expeditiously transported to an 'invaded' coastal town by motor vehicles. The town chosen was Hastings, and W & G du Cros contributed with a score of their new Napier chassis fitted by them with hastily constructed lorry bodies. W & G supplied civilian drivers from their staff.

In 1910 a number of Panhard-Levassor taxicabs were put into service and a showroom for that maker's cars was opened at 177 The Vale. Hundreds of the new cabs, smartly turned out, with tyres white-washed, bright yellow bonnets, and gleaming brass radiators, lamps and

W & G badges, could be seen on the taxi ranks at Ealing Broadway Station and Holland Park or cruising in the West End in the hands of drivers in smart dark green uniforms. The public were quick to recognise their extra comfort and speed. Business was good. The drivers were paid twenty-five shillings weekly. Although that seemed average at that time, the men were not satisfied with other conditions and somehow du Cros gained the reputation for being bad employers. In January 1913 the drivers (as well as some others employed by different firms) called a strike which dragged on for weeks, then months. At a meeting of the management, the general manager, Mr W A Turpin, expressed the view that the stoppage was bringing the firm near to disaster and that the loss of takings from a thousand taxicabs proved it was folly to have 'all their eggs in one basket'. He further suggested they should run a van hire business similar to that of Thomas Tilling. He also saw scope in the parcel carrying business.

After the strike had ended, the Turpin formula was put into practice with a number of cab bodies being removed from the 15hp Napier chassis and light van bodies built on them. By midsummer, a fleet of 100 vans of one ton capacity, fitted with Dunlop pneumatic tyres all round,

A view of the overhauling department at W & G du Cros' Acton works in 1914.

A view of the overhauling department at W & G du Cros' Acton works in 1914.

The first W & G 1½ and 2 ton trucks available to other operators in 1919.

were operating a parcels carrying service. Painted the now familiar green with yellow bonnet and road wheels, on the sides a large W & G sign in script with the words 'Express Carriers', the body was open at the rear end where a youthful vanguard held on to a rope. These vans seemed to be the fastest in London at that time and their nippy getaway and manoeuvrability of the taxicab chassis was fully exploited by the drivers.

I have the memory of these vans racing along the street with the road wheels looking like yellow catherine wheels. They could slam to a stop, the van guard-boy would have the packages on the tail ready, while the driver made a marvellously rapid three point turn. Then the driver would dash into the consignee's premises with the goods. Thus the W & G express carrier service was a great success with these fast, light vans, particularly as at this time the established carriers, Carter Paterson, Pickfords, Suttons and the railway companies were using mainly horse transport, while their motor vehicles were heavier and used solid tyres which legally restricted their speed to 12 miles per hour. By the autumn of 1913 several hundred W & G vans were serving an area of suburban London, including Bromley, Dartford, Romford, Redhill, Watford, Waltham Cross and Egham.

A city depôt was opened in Watling Street enabling a four hourly collection and delivery there. A large central depôt was opened in Pakenham Street, Clerkenwell, facilitating quicker sorting and distribution of goods to the commercial centres of London. This depôt was served by feeder vans which plied to and from Acton Vale. Amongst these were Albions, heavier Napiers, a 5 ton Milnes-Daimler,

fitted with a radiator and bonnet from an X-type LGOC bus and a large W & G built body, and a 3 ton Panhard of an early type with a flat topped bonnet and trapezium shaped radiator, chain driven, wood wheels and solid twin tyres at the rear. I often saw it grinding along Bayswater Road, heavily laden on its evening run to Clerkenwell. The popularity of the carrier service was

such that vans were still loading for evening deliveries up to 5.30 pm at Pakenham Street.

Early in 1914 W & G du Cros embarked on their van hire service. Premises for this were acquired at Regency Street, Westminster. The same type of Napier vans were used, painted in the hirer's own choice of livery, with du Cros supplying the drivers. Cheap rates combined with

Two coaches and a bus, all with twenty seats and based on the 2 ton chassis, supplied in 1923 by Frank Hopper and Sons Ltd of Glasgow, W & G's Scottish distributors.

A 1923 advertisement showing a variety of bodywork on 2 and 2½ ton chassis.

good maintenance made this a popular feature. Many leading London businesses placed contracts. Among them were W H Smith & Son, who hired a fleet in their then familiar red and gold colours, Wyman & Son, the booksellers, Nevill's Bread, Mudie's Library, Sangers of Euston, the wholesale chemists, whose vans advertised their 'Glymiel Jelly', the Gaumont Film Company, as well as *The Daily Graphic* and *The Observer* newspapers. Some companies at this time were favouring a change from horse transport without the problems of ownership of motor vehicles, and the W & G hire arrangements suited them admirably.

By March of 1914, hundreds of Napier vans, in addition to the large fleet of taxicabs, were on the London streets earning good money for the du Cros firm. The warm summer of that year passed uneventfully until August. Then came the war.

Britain was quite unprepared for this dire emergency in which armies would have to be moved quickly. The Army Service Corps was still equipped with the GS wagons as used in the Boer War fourteen years earlier, with horses and mules to haul them.

Officials from the War Office, armed with requisition documents, visited all users of large numbers of motor vehicles of the required standards. The success of the Napiers at the Hastings exercise five years previously had no doubt suitably impressed Whitehall, resulting in the whole W & G fleet being commandeered for war service. I remember seeing hundreds of Napiers parked in echelon in Hyde Park and Kensington Gardens

around October 1914, some still with stickers on the windscreen with the words 'Kitchener Wants You'. The vehicles were soon shipped to France which must have left the W & G garages bare indeed. The Panhard cabs I seem to remember were not taken, but sold to individual operators. The Pakenham Street depôt was taken by Carter Paterson, the carriers, and the Acton Vale workshops embarked on war work. Napiers nearby were producing 30 cwt, 2 ton and 3 ton lorries for the Army. Later in the war, W & G produced a 30 cwt lorry similar in outline to that of Napier, fitted with a 4 cylinder 85 x 130mm engine (of uncertain provenance, possibly Dorman. Certainly by 1920 it had grown to 95 x 140 and was by Dorman and claimed to be made exclusively for W & G, who placed an early order for 300 engines). The familiar initials W & G were embossed on the aluminium radiator casing of the new truck, surely the first time that a vehicle was named after its backer's Christian names in this way.

This truck grew from a pre-war intention by W & G to make their own distribution vehicles. They had built a few experimental chassis from 1914 onwards that had given good service, and by the time that production versions were announced for general release in 1919, Carter Paterson had already decided to adopt them as their standard light lorries to work alongside their heavier Leylands. If a decision to make vehicles sounds to be over optimistic, one

A selection of W & G customers' vehicles supplied up to 1925. How many they sold is uncertain but an early one was chassis no 10032, suggesting that the series began at 10000 and a late 1924 or early 1925 one was chassis no 10606.

should not forget du Cros' enormous practical experience with running vehicles. They did all their own bodybuilding and maintenance work and even made all their own spare parts. The Acton works had vast machine shops, wood working tools, paint shops and stores. In early 1914

they employed no less than 3000 men, had over 130,000 gallons of petrol in store and even had their own wells able to supply 150,000 gallons of water a day primarily for vehicle washing.

Just six weeks after the end of the war, on 21st December 1918, came the death of William Harvey du Cros at the age of seventy-two in his native Dublin. Not only had he created the firm of Dunlop, but he had been awarded France's premier award, the *Legion d'Honneur*, for his

services to industry. He had been chairman of the RAC and as a final tribute on his semi-retirement, he had been elected first and only president of Dunlop.

Arthur succeeded him as MP for Hastings, and in 1919 was created a baronet. Outside the main entrance of the Warple Way building, a three foot high stone pillar was set at the kerbside, inscribed thus: 'To William Harvey du Cros. Founder of the Pneumatic Tyre industry'. The stone stood for many years after the

demise of the firm of du Cros. Meanwhile, in 1919, W & G uprated the 30 cwt to a 2 tonner and in 1920 introduced a 2½ ton version with four instead of three forward gears. These sold well and could be seen around the country in good numbers. In London, caterers Joseph Lyons bought a fleet of them, as did Army & Navy Stores, Oliver Dring, the sausage purveyors, Shell, BP, Pratts, Carter Paterson, Pickfords and Star Laundry of Hackney. Quite a number were made with bus

and charabanc bodies, including some as early as 1920 with pneumatic tyres, electric lighting and self starters. A 1921 curiosity was the W & G Three Purpose Body, which was a screw tipper or platform lorry which carried five stowed away benches which could be bolted down (partly to stop it being inadvertently tipped!) and then carry thirty passengers. By 1924 this vehicle was called the Chara-tipper and quite a few were sold for carrying miners and coal in South Wales and the

Sheffield area. Another 1921 vehicle was the Way-Tip which was again intended for coal and could tip a small amount either to left or right by hand-hydraulics and weigh it as it fell into a sack.

The chassis of all these vehicles were conventional but with nice detail touches which showed the operating experience that had gone into them. The rear axles were located by torque brackets, the frame rails were 'inside out' to aid the replacement of cross bearers

Shown at the 1923 Commercial Motor Show was this W & G 2½ tonner, fitted with two gravity tipping Makrob skips. Other exhibits were a 20 seat Bartle bodied bus and a two ton truck. W & G also made £95 all-steel four ton trailers that year. The chassis of the two ton truck cost £440 and the 2½ tonner £490.

The early style of W & G chassis, photographed in 1923, with 'inside-out' frame, 22.4hp Dorman engine and torque rod located rear axle.

Though W & G built much of their own bodywork, this two tonner was equipped by Bayleys. What can be seen of the radiator badge suggests that it is 1923 or later, as W & G is flanked by 'London' and 'Du Cros' [presumably for symmetry, they used a capital D on their badge].

without dismantling the chassis, lock nuts were used throughout and aluminium was used as a bulkhead support and rubbing strip between the chassis and bonnet sides.

In the early twenties W & G du Cros also retained their Panhard agency and exhibited 30 cwt - 3 ton models at Olympia in apparent competition to their own vehicles, and of course they also continued the taxi business. In 1922 none other than Sunbeam wizard Louis Coatalen was reported to be designing a new taxi chassis for them (presumably for them to build themselves) but nothing seems to have come of this, nor of plans to import Talbot Darracq chassis to be fitted with W & G bodywork, and in 1924 a new venture started instead. A fleet of 100 cabs of the American type we saw on films at the time began operating in London in the name of W & G. The cabs were made by the Canadian Yellow Cab Co of Orrilla, Ontario, shipped over to England in packing cases and assembled by W & G at Acton, both for themselves and for Europe, a hundred being sold to Berlin in 1925. These cabs, with their 15.9 or 18.3hp 4 cylinder Continental engines, were in a new livery of orange and black with disc wheels, and had electric lighting, rubber blocks on spring ends and rear springs slung under the axle. They were upholstered in crocodile leather with interior lights that lit on opening the doors, and had CYC badges as well as W & G on their radiators.

The cabs were operated by the Turpin Engineering Co from 15 London Road, Acton Vale, part of the original du Cros workshops. This firm had been registered in 1901 as a Panhard agent and from the mid-twenties was the vehicle operating side of W & G. A later director, along with W A Turpin, was Major Vitty, chief engineer to the Metropolitan Police until 1930.

The orange cabs vanished from the London scene as suddenly as they had appeared. I was told by a cabbie at the time that they failed on account of the English, unlike the Americans, preferring a cab of more

A 1926 advertisement for the L model. The order referred to from the MAB was for an ambulance/coach with 28 seats and doors to each row.

The first nine of a fleet of 100 Yellow Cabs, both assembled and operated by W & G in 1924. They, or rather the Yellow Cab Manufacturing Co of England Ltd, also supplied similar vehicles to Berlin in 1925. All had Continental engines, full electrics and very soft springing. It seems that they were too garish for London travellers.

sombre appearance. I do remember some of the orange cabs being repainted dark blue with the W & G initials, so this may have been so.

Mention of Louis Coatalen in connection with an abortive W & G taxi design must now make us retrace our steps to 1920 and the formation of the Sunbeam-Talbot-Darracq combine. What few people may realise is that this should, by rights, have been called STDW&G, as the fourth member of the group, following Darracq's acquisition of Clément Talbot in London in 1919, and their subsequent amalgamation in 1920 with Sunbeam, was W & G du Cros Ltd. One can only assume that the death of financier and company promoter W H du Cros in 1918 had made this move a necessity - indeed it is quite possible that his holdings were also tied up in the British owned French Darracq concern in view of his earlier friendship with Monsieur Darracq, and involvement in the French motor industry.

In exchange for all the issued W & G shares, holders (probably mainly the du Cros family and W A Turpin) received 7% of the shares in STD Motors Ltd, whilst James Todd, STD chairman, spoke of the advantages of the W & G bodyworks to the new group.

However, to return to W & G products once more, there was a new 20/24 seat bus in April 1924 using a virtually standard truck chassis and a new style of almost Talbot shaped radiator. A little over a year later came a true drop frame bus (1ft 10in laden chassis height) with a six cylinder 33.5 RAC hp engine, front wheel brakes and a top speed of 55 mph. It came out in October, just two weeks earlier than the first of the famous low frame Gilfords, whose specification closely mirrored it. 1925 was, of course, the great year of the drop frame, after the lead taken by the NS and Maudslay, but the London built W & G and Gilford were unusual in using American six cylinder monobloc engines - by Continental and Buda respectively. The L model, as the W & G passenger chassis became known, carried on into the thirties and was listed in buyers' guides until, at any rate, 1933. It was supplemented by the M model in August 1928, which appears to have retained the same engine but with an extra 1/8 inch in

An early W & G rubs shoulders with some bigger vehicles [and bigger names - Leyland and Tilling-Stevens] in W B Dick & Co Ltd's Ilo Lubricants fleet.

This 1928 Talbot advertisement poses a number of tricky questions. Why were W & G, appointed the marketers of all Talbot commercials in 1927, not mentioned if both firms were still members of STD? If W & G were no longer members then Talbot's lorry might be logical, but it does not explain why Talbot, and not W & G, made 30 cwt Subsidy trucks in 1922 when both were certainly associated? Apparently Talbot abandoned the Subsidy design when a four figure order from the WD turned out to be for only 200.

the bore, whilst the L, at this stage, was reduced in price and now had a six cylinder 6JUL Dorman 100 x 140mm engine, which at some stage was also adopted by the M. Most of these Ls/Ms were supplied to East Midlands operators, to Bourne-mouth Corporation Tramways, who also used Dorman engines in their Karrier fleet, and to South Wales, where Jefferys & Co Ltd of Wassail Square Garage, Swansea, were distributors. Jefferys sold no less than 72 W & Gs of all types, but

especially psv's (including over 20 to Llanelly Express) in two years from an initial £40,000 order in August 1924. Unfortunately, many of their operators were hit by the Depression and Jefferys had to bail several out before they severed their connections with W & G and became successful Tilling-Stevens distributors. Both the L and M were available (though few were built) with forward control, when they became the LF and MF respectively. Chris Taylor estimates that around 175 Ls and its deriva-tives were made, plus perhaps 45 of a new four cylinder 20 seater in the 11,500 chassis number series intro-duced in 1927. In that same year, Turpin Engineering ran 24 new fleet name W & G Safety Coaches on a daily service between London and Bognor, as well as regular trips to Brighton, Bournemouth and Ilfra-combe. Whether this was to make use of unsold vehicles or to convince other operators of their worth is unknown, but before long this oper-ating side of the W & G empire fizzled out.

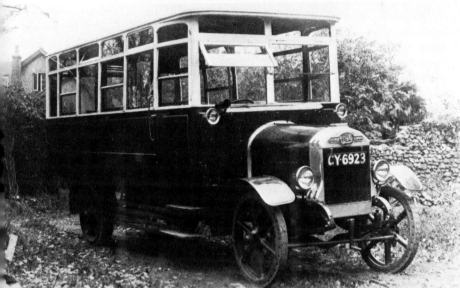

Alongside the fast bus and coach chassis came a new 30 cwt truck in April 1925 with an angular radiator and the lettering 'du Cros' and 'London' cast either side of 'W & G', as had first appeared on the psv's in 1923. It had a 95 x 130mm four cylinder engine of distinctly American appearance, an in-unit four speed gearbox, a Kirkstall worm drive rear axle and a more conventional frame with the flanges pointing inwards and no torque rods.

More interesting, from a technical viewpoint, was the Metropolitan Asylums Board ambulance, in which W & G became involved and of which one example is fortunately preserved by the London Ambulance Service. The MAB ambulance came about as a result of dissatisfaction with existing types, which were too high and uncomfortable.

Since about 1920 the MAB had run Talbots with twin rear wheels based on Great War designs and Crossleys of similarly antiquated origins. In December 1925 the MAB's Major Huddart decided to build a specimen vehicle incorporating his requirements and this appeared a year later with 27.3hp six cylinder Continental engine angled offset to the nearside so that it could drive to a differential mounted close to the nearside rear wheel, thus leaving a low central gangway in best bus traditions. Interested firms were invited to tender for the privilege of making production versions and in March 1927 W & G's quote of £695 for each of fifteen chassis was accepted, to be fitted with bodywork by the MAB. The vehicle was fast, stable and comfortable and, apart from the first Continental engined version, was always fitted with a six cylinder Meadows 3¼ litre engine, as found in contemporary Invictas and the six cylinder Bean car amongst others. Its rear axle was, incidentally, a Kirkstall casing with gears cut by W & G. By all accounts the MAB E type ambulance was produced until 1936 and was occasionally sold to individual hospitals or Health Boards outside London.

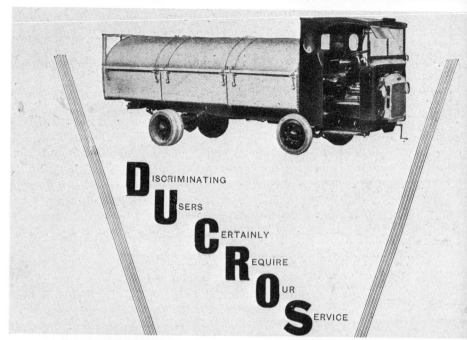

On 1st April 1930 the MAB (whose first vehicle had been a steam Thornycroft in 1902, followed by Dennis, Belsize, Siddeley-Deasy and Daimler before the twenties) was merged by the LCC with the London Ambulance Service and the Metropolitan Board of Guardians. Previously, the LAS had been concerned with street accidents, the MBG with its own hospitals, and the MAB with fever patients. No sooner were LCC ambulances on the street than a switch was made back to Talbot vehicles, this time the advanced six cylinder 75 chassis specially adapted for ambulance work by the provision of a double reduction rear axle to give low axle height. Later, the 90 engine was also used, along with adjustable shock absorbers and a pre-select gearbox, to give a most refined and impressive performance.

W & G du Cros and Talbot were probably still linked at that stage and, in 1927, W & G had become responsible for the marketing of all Talbot commercial vehicles. Curiously enough, when Talbot introduced a new 30 cwt commercial chassis in 1928, no mention of W & G was made in its advertisements - in fact, Fitch McGillivray & Co Ltd of Shaftesbury Avenue were described as London distributors. It seems quite possible that the MAB contract was not all that profitable to W & G, because not only did the orders become smaller (13 in 1928 and only 6 in 1929, the last year W & G orders for the MAB are mentioned) but the price per chassis came down from £695 to £635 in 1928 and £620 in the following year. In an effort to stir up some more orders from a different source, the ambulance chassis was lengthened and demonstrated to seaside municipalities early in 1928 as a promenade bus. To make this Jekyll and Hyde transformation of what, after all, was supposed to be a dashing vehicle, W & G installed a two speed transfer box under the floor which in high ratio gave 25 mph at 1000 rpm in top gear but only 10 at the same revs of its Meadows engine when a flap was lifted and low range selected. It retained the horseshoe-shaped MAB radiator and whether many of these EL models were sold seems highly debatable.

A popular area in which failing truck manufacturers sought solace was in municipal vehicles, where orders tended to be for batches of vehicles and financial constraints were less than in the cut and thrust world of general haulage. W & G were no exception, and having invented a self dumping dustcart trailer in 1926, they went on to make small wheeled Freighters in 1929 of a type then very much the rage for municipal work. These came with both forward and normal control in the W & G range for loads of up to 3 tons. They had the four cylinder Meadows 4EK and 4EL engines, though Meadows' sales records suggest that very few can have been made. In addition to engines, Meadows supplied gearboxes to W & G and records show that 32 were ordered in 1929, 18 in 1930, 7 in 1931, 5 in 1932 and then only 2 up to April 1934 when a final 2 more were ordered. Of course, this does not necessarily constitute total W & G vehicle sales as there is no means of knowing which models used this gearbox. Of the six cylinder Meadows engines of the MAB type, 22 went to W & G in 1927, 20 in 1928 and 7 in the first five months of 1929 which, related to MAB orders, can perhaps be taken to mean that only 14 MAB type chassis went to outside customers - certainly one went to Harrogate Infirmary in 1929. Interestingly enough, one of these engines in 1928 accidentally shared the same serial number as a similar engine supplied to Brocklebank, the obscure subject of a recent article in *OLD MOTOR*, and by then on their last legs and presumably not assembling their own engines any more.

In September 1927 a new and more robust 2½ ton W & G had appeared with a right hand in place of the centre gate change used on its predecessor (a strange deviation from contemporary trends) and very thick aluminium radiator sides that tapered outwards to conceal the clamping down bolts. A fleet of these

London and was a multi-millionaire. He owned the lovely mansion known as *Canons* at Edgware, which stood on the site of the former palace of the Duke of Chandos nearly 200 years previously. *Canons* was set in 240 acres of parkland with lakes, stretching back from the Edgware Road to Marsh Lane in Stanmore. Sir Arthur sold this estate to the famous property tycoon Mr George Cross in 1925, as described in Mr Cross' book *Suffolk Punch*, for £150,000. The house and surrounding grounds were purchased by North London Collegiate School in 1929. The Stanmore end was later developed by D C Estates. Sir Arthur also owned the palatial Craigwell House in Bognor, which he made available for the convalescence of King George V after his serious illness in 1929, after which the town became known as Bognor Regis.

Sir Arthur du Cros lost much of his wealth in the £13 million shares crash for which company promoter Clarence Hatry was jailed for 14 years in 1930. Sir Arthur, then aged 72, was residing in his elegant town house at Park Place, St James, surrounded by priceless antiques.

In his retirement in the South of France, he set down a record of the birth of the Dunlop empire, which was published in 1938 under the title *Wheels of Fortune*. Unfortunately, his book makes virtually no reference to du Cros interests outside the tyre industry and the only reference to W & G is that they ran a fleet of cabs. William is described as having died in 1937, though George was presumably still alive at the time the book was written. Sir Arthur's son was a barrister, so plainly not involved in the motor industry and which, if any, of the du Cros brothers were still involved with Dunlop is not mentioned.

It seems that the du Cros' disappearance from the motor industry was almost as complete as their arrival had been spectacular in Victorian times; but as proof that they actually existed, one only has to look at the photographs of the W & G truck that has come to light in Australia, plus the preserved MAB ambulance, and see the street names on Canons Park Estate at Edgware, *viz*: du Cros Drive, Howbery Road and Cornbury Road, after the two country homes of William Harvey, and the little street in Acton Vale named du Cros Road, which bordered the only one of the du Cros family's motor factories which actually bore their illustrious name.

2½ tonners was used to transport Pratts petrol, whilst another well known user was Pickfords who, in 1929, inexplicably ordered a 30 cwt W & G with a De Lavaud free wheeling back axle controlled from the steering column.

1929 marked W & G's last appearance at the London Commercial Motor Show, when they exhibited an ambulance, a forward control all weather coach with H E Taylor bodywork, a 30 cwt laundry van and two refuse collectors (one of which was for Acton). What happened after that is obscured by the mists of time. W & G appeared in buyers' guides up to 1934 and then again in 1935, when only the MAB ambulance was listed, from a new address and by a new company, W & G Ltd of Seagrave Road (where Renault resided), London W6. If W & G was still part of the STD combine, then this is perhaps explained quite easily

by the group's collapse in that year and the possible rescue of odd bits of it that did not appeal to Rootes by other parties. At this stage, the Talbot ambulance chassis was priced at £420 (75) and £450 (90) and ironically it survived the Rootes take-over by a couple of years.

Possibly the W & G ambulance lasted even longer. Certainly, W & G Ltd still existed in November 1939, because Chris Taylor has a piece of their letterhead to prove it, which mentions that they are motor and general engineers and manufacturers of W & G ambulances, etc. Perhaps the full story will never be known, which seems odd for so mighty a motor industry family, which entered the transport industry in such a major way and disappeared from it with hardly a murmur. And what of the remaining du Cros sons?

Sir Arthur du Cros, eldest of them, had served as Lord Mayor of

# 'IF NO ONE ELSE MAKES IT DOUGLAS CAN'

When others simply bought and sold ex military vehicles, Leslie Douglas put his years
in the truck industry to good use with special AEC Matador conversions.
From these grew an astonishingly diverse range
of custom built Douglas trucks in the fifties
that finally gave way to the airport and terminal Tugmasters so familiar today.

A 6x6 version of the original Logger was available from around 1950 and here one is put through its paces at a military vehicle test site in Hampshire.

This early Douglas badge reminds one of timber vehicle origins - no doubt it is a Douglas fir log!

The Douglas Logger tractor changed little in appearance between 1947 and the mid-fifties. Starting as a Matador conversion it was completely built by Douglas from new parts by the time this military example was made. Douglas also made pole trailers to go with their tractors.

ONE of the lesser known truck makers of the forties, fifties and sixties was F L Douglas (Equipment) Ltd of Cheltenham. They may never have been a major name in the industry but what they lacked in quantity they more than made up for in unusual designs. Indeed, the company philosophy became 'if it runs on rubber tyres and isn't made anywhere else, then Douglas can tackle it'.

They would still be making 'specials' today but for two specials they introduced in the fifties and which soon expanded to the exclusion of all else - terminal tractors and aircraft tugs. Indeed, Douglas Lowe, the General Manager, assured me that if times ever became hard they could still turn their hands to purpose-built trucks - but there seems no likelihood of that with the 137 employees busily hand-building ten elevating fifth wheel tractors and half a dozen air tugs each month.

How did it all start? Well, Frank Leslie Douglas had worked for over twenty years selling heavy vehicles before he started his own firm in 1947. He had previously worked for Armstrong-Saurer and then Unipower, whose 4x4 logging tractors had first appeared in 1937 as a sideline to their principal business of converting two axle trucks to six wheelers to increase their payload.

Douglas put his experience of logging vehicles into special AEC Matador conversions. The Matadors were bought in Ministry sales and reconditioned where necessary. If not already fitted, they were equipped with powerful winches and fold-down jibs to aid timber extraction and loading. The original build cards are lost and chassis numbering has always run from 1-999 and then each time returned to the beginning again. However, the timber tractors were plainly a success, as the number still in use today testifies, and a grand total of over 4000 Douglas trucks (excluding Tugmasters) of all types was eventually built.

With their Converter rear bogie and modified chassis, Douglas were able to convert mass-produced trucks into cheap and flexible off-road transporters. This Austin dated from 1954 and was Douglas' DM4 model type. They also converted Austin Loadstars to 4x4.

Another conversion, this time a 'Big Bedford' to six wheel drive for the Army. Similar vehicles were made by Douglas on the later pattern, Bedford S and also the TK.

Normal control versions of the original Matador and Militant type vehicles were also made. This is a DH 66 18/20 ton tractor with 125 bhp AEC diesel, and Douglas transfer box and axles.

The 1954 DM 64 Transporter employed many Leyland components with Douglas' own single leaf spring trunnion bogie. It could carry ten ton up a 1 in 2.5 gradient. A four wheel conversion on the same chassis was one of the first Tugmasters.

As the supply of Matadors in good order dried up, so Leslie Douglas found himself having to make more and more of the vehicles himself, buying in the bulk of the new components from AEC as he went along. By 1950 he was offering the 9.6 litre AEC engined Logger chassis, as it was called, as the Transporter and Prospector for general off-road haulage and oil well drilling respectively. A 6x6 Transporter was also available for 22 ton gvw operation and a year later this was offered with engines of up to 250 bhp, 6x2 (front wheel drive), 6x4 or 6x6 drive, forward or normal control. Douglas were also making their winches for fitment to various other types of vehicle as well as lightweight bogies with two axle drive for fitment to a variety of chassis.

The range had by now expanded to fire and crash tender chassis and rotary snow plough carriers with eight cylinder Rolls-Royce petrol engines. Much of the output was exported or built for government

Several oilfield conversions of Commer Super-poise chassis were built for W J Reynolds [Motors] Ltd, Dagenham. This one dates from 1957 and was classed as a Douglas DL6 7/10 tonner. Note the tropical cab roof skin and the extra ventilation in the front of the bonnet.

Commer became the most common make for Douglas 4x4, 6x4 and 6x6 conversions and were called the C series when forward control and D series when normal control. This C of c1959 was for the Libyan Army, one of around 25 countries to have bought Douglas vehicles at that stage. Wm Press, the civil engineers, had one of the largest fleets of Douglas - over 80 - and mainly Commer based.

Note the massive chassis on this 150 bhp DH 64 designed to withstand winch loading of heavy oilfield equipment over its rear. It could carry 25 tons and in this instance had a wheelbase of 22 feet.

departments, local authorities and petrol companies.

1954 saw the start of what was to become the firm's speciality when they converted a bonneted Leyland Comet into a Tugmaster DM4 for Silver City Airways. The Leyland cab and engine were retained but the wheelbase was dramatically shortened to reduce the turning circle to 30 feet. The rear axle was mounted rigidly and the gear ratios altered to give from 1.77 to 21 mph at maximum engine torque in first and fifth (top) gears respectively. Tractive effort was 11,400 lbs which meant that up to 40 tons could be towed.

The Comet also provided the basis for lighter DM64 (6x4) and DM6 (6x6) Transporters with the usual 90 bhp Leyland engine. These were fitted with a transfer box to give ten forward gears from 1.3 to 35 mpg at optimum torque. They could climb

How today's Tugmaster terminal tractor with its elevating fifth wheel began - a 1955 Tugmaster destined for Venezuela, demonstrating its ability to match a giant oilfield trailer.

Douglas made crane carrier chassis from the mid-fifties with 6x4 or 6x6. This is a fifteen ton capacity TK 66, one of a number built for Priestman as the basis for their Caribou crane. It had the Perkins R6 108 bhp diesel and a two ratio, six speed gearbox, giving a 120:1 bottom gear. Rear suspension was by solid beams pivoting from central trunnions.

A fleet of DM/4DC Prospectors bound for Shell in Venezuela about 1957. They are equipped with self loading platforms or drilling mud tanks. Some also carried drilling rigs.

1 in 2.5 gradients ,with ten tons aboard and utilised the Douglas bogie with its centre trunnion suspension that allowed 9 inches of articulation to each rear wheel before it lost traction. Subsequently, Douglas struck up a relationship with Commer and most 4x4, 6x4 and 6x6 medium weight conversions henceforth used their components. Unipower were doing much the same, with an emphasis on Dodge chassis at the time, whilst Vickers-AWD were soon to join the fray, often using Ford components. A N Davis, the designer at Douglas, went to AWD in 1954 and was replaced by John Carroll, the current managing director at Douglas, who had previously worked for Dowty Hydraulics in Cheltenham. Leslie Douglas was always very much an innovator - dreaming up applications for winches and special vehicles that he could go out and find a customer for. Understandably, this sometimes led to more model types than customers.

A post hole borer, powered by Super Major engine, at work in North Wales for MAN-WEB. It is mounted on a DM66 chassis.

A Swiss-made Aebi snow-blower on a 130 bhp petrol engined Douglas carrier. It could clear heavy accumulations of snow at the rate of 300 yards per hour in the lowest of its eight gears and travel between drifts at up to 30 mph.

Probably one of the last big Prospector 25 ton chassis of around 1960 looking now more like a Leyland or Scammell than an AEC. This is a DH64 with 250 bhp Cummins or Rolls-Royce diesel and six speed manual gearbox or automatic transmission.

As well as the Comet-based Tugmaster, Douglas made a Rolls-Royce 5.6 litre eight cylinder engined tractor which could cope with all-up weights of almost 300,000 lbs and this was joined by a whole range of Tugmasters down to 8000 lbs tractive effort with choice of two or four wheel drive on most of the models. The first elevating fifth wheel tractor for use with semi-trailers of all heights was built in 1955 for export to Venezuela, and these gradually became a mainstay of the firm.

The old AEC-based Transporters with forward or normal control were still being made and the bonneted 4x2 four wheeler was enjoying some success as a fifteen ton capacity dumptruck. On the strength of this, a forward control, half cab, 4x4 version was developed in 1959, called the 944. This used the Commer TS3 two stroke 105 bhp diesel and two range four speed gearbox and, with a 6/9 cubic yard body, it had a payload of 21,160 lbs. Oversize rear tyres (15.00 x 20 as against 11.00 x

A natural extension to Douglas' growing air tug business was this Cargomaster aircraft loader. Production versions used four hydraulic posts instead of scissors and a Tugmaster type half cab which allowed the conveyor belt to lie alongside it.

Storming up a loose surfaced 1 in 2 gradient, a 1957 Pathfinder with 85 bhp Rootes petrol engine shows off its Douglas designed independent front suspension. A Tugmaster version of the same basic vehicle was also available for aircraft of up to 130,000 lbs.

Built for industrial handling or logging, this is the DC44 four wheel steer tractor with 25,000 lb winch and land anchor. This vehicle is believed to have been bought by British Rail about 1961, and had a Commer two stroke diesel.

And now for something completely different - a Douglas bus! Dating from the mid-fifties, it was bodied in South Africa and had a four cylinder Meadows diesel, though a handful of others had 6 cyl Meadows.

20 on the front) were standard and a two wheel drive version was also offered. Thos W Ward Ltd, with branches at Sheffield, London, Glasgow, Coventry and Briton Ferry were appointed sole distributors and within a couple of years the machine had been renamed the Automaster 8 and was the smallest of a whole new range of Automasters in 1960. The larger models, the 15 and 22 (capacity in tons) had a number of unusual features, including (probably for the first time in Britain) automatic SCG gearbox with torque converter and widely

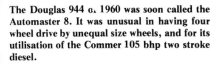

The Douglas 944 of 1960 was soon called the Automaster 8. It was unusual in having four wheel drive by unequal size wheels, and for its utilisation of the Commer 105 bhp two stroke diesel.

Largest of the Automasters was the 22 [its load in tons]. It had turbocharged 250 bhp diesels by Rolls-Royce or Cummins and an SCG epicyclic gearbox with 3:1 torque converter to allow two pedal control. The low height and compact wheelbase were important sales points though production ended soon after the reorganisation of Douglas in 1962.

In 1962 and 1963 Douglas made both 4x4 and 6x6 trucks based on Commer components. They were used by Esso Research for spraying the desert in Tunisia with an oil by-product that stabilised the sand for planting.

Douglas Firefly fire crash tender chassis with Sun equipment supplied to the Ministry of Transport and Civil Aviation in 1958. They had Rolls-Royce 196 bhp petrol engines and automatic transmissions. Top speed was 60 mph and the Douglas full torque pto originally developed for timber winching worked the pump.

Another unusual type of Douglas, again for South Africa. Built for the Johannesburg Fire Dept, this DM42 chassis was bodied by Carmichael & Sons [Worcester] Ltd. It had a 196 bhp Rolls-Royce petrol engine, automatic transmission and a top speed of 60 mph.

copied body design which incorporated a built-in subframe that helped to reduce overall height by ten inches. Like the 'little' Automaster 8 the six wheelers had half cabs, but instead of a flush-mounted radiator the whole engine compartment continued forward of the cab and front axle by several feet, giving a

An interesting 4x4 vehicle supplied in 1963 for factory maintenance. It had a crew compartment and workshop as well as a hydraulic platform.

Douglas built prototype motorway snowplough/gritters for the MoT when the M1 opened. This Douglas dates from 1960 and had an eight cylinder Rolls-Royce petrol engine. Production versions were produced by Atkinson and Scammell.

Looking like a cross between an Automaster 8 and a Foden, that is exactly what this is. Fodens won the order from Guernsey in 1963 but found that all their models were too wide to meet island laws, so they gave Douglas a kit of parts for them to build a one-off dumptruck.

tight turning circle at the expense of a curious appearance.

The Automaster 15 used the 178 bhp Rolls-Royce C6NFL diesel with the option of Cummins HU170B or Leyland 680 and the 22 used the Cummins NT6 or Rolls-Royce C6T, both producing 250 bhp.

For a time, until replaced by Tugmasters, the dumptrucks were an important part of the firm, which even formed a new subsidiary, Douglas Dump Trucks Ltd, at their new factory in Arle Rd, Cheltenham. (Incidentally, the firm had already been split into Douglas All Wheel Drive Vehicles Ltd and Douglas Equipment Ltd in 1956 but appears to have gone back to its old title later - certainly it was F L Douglas Equipment Ltd from 1961 when it was reformed by Leslie Douglas after an unsuccessful spell as part of a furniture to finance group that went bust. Incidentally, Ted Croker, well known today as secretary to the Football Association, was sales director for two years up to the reformation. Some dumptrucks were exported, including one that was driven overland to Spain in 1962 by the demonstration driver, an unpleasant prospect when one considers the heavy duty springs and top speed in the thirties. Thos W Ward Ltd sold some Automaster 8s to the National Coal Board and one order came from a most unexpected source - Fodens Ltd of Sandbach. It was for Guernsey, where width restrictions ruled out a standard Foden model but Douglas were able to build one using Foden parts wherever possible.

This talk of dump trucks has taken us a little ahead of our story because some other interesting special types had been developed in the mid-fifties, notably a lighter Prospector with P6 Perkins diesel, the 25/30 cwt Pathfinder and some large 6x4 and 6x6 112 to 150 bhp half cab chassis for mobile cranes and excavators, examples of which were supplied to Priestman and the Air Ministry. A contemporary catalogue shows that the Prospector was almost anything you wanted it to be, including a normal control 4x4 or 6x6 with Airflow Streamlines

Commer-shape cab, a forward control 4x4 with Commer cab, a 4x4 or 6x6 with Douglas' own normal control cab, either looking like the old AEC-derived design or like the latest Leyland Super Hippo! Engines of 112 to 250 bhp were discussed along with payloads of 2-25 tons.

The Pathfinder was an uncharacteristically small truck for Douglas and one which was used primarily for oil exploration, particularly by BP who built up a small fleet of them. The cab was an Airflow Streamlines normal control design and there was a choice of Rootes six cylinder petrol or Perkins P6 diesel, both developing 85 bhp. A two ratio, four speed gearbox gave from 1.65 mph (1.4 mph petrol)to 47 mph (60 mph petrol) at optimum engine torque. Tractive effort was 10,000 lbs and a front mounted 6000 lb winch was available.

On road test in 1957, *Modern Transport*, '*The Times* of the Transport World', covered roughly 12 miles per gallon and commented on its extremely good ride both on and off the road. The explanation for this was independent front suspension by coil springs and unequal length wishbones pivoting from the centrally mounted spiral bevel gear housing. Though equipped with a normal live back axle and semi-elliptic springs, it was intended to fit independent rear suspension on future examples. Special hubs enabled double tyres to be fitted all round to improve flotation, especially on sand.

Special products in the late fifties and early sixties were gradually phased out by the growing volume of tug and tractor orders but before they disappeared some remarkable orders were undertaken. There was a crane carrier type chassis to carry the cleaning machinery for the roof of the Mersey Tunnel. It replaced a

**Whilst Douglas' special vehicles are interesting to see, one should not lose sight of the fact that, after 1962, nearly all their production was of Tugmasters for docks and airports. This is a typical elevating fifth wheel terminal tractor of 1966, towing a Swedish U-frame container handler at Southampton.**

**The unusual front wheel drive truck with its mechanically raised body, built for Bofors in 1962, that was subsequently supplied to Bristol-Siddeley after it was found to be too heavy for a bridge in Sweden.**

thirty year old Pagefield chassis and is believed to be in use to this day. Various fire appliance and crash tender chassis were produced, notably for Johannesburg, Beirut and the British Ministry of Transport and Civil Aviation, who took a number of distinctly Nubian-type six wheelers in 1958. Then there were 4x4 rotary snow plough chassis sold for both road and airfield duties, plus a small batch of 196 bhp Rolls-

With their wide experience of container handling Tugmasters, it is perhaps not surprising that Douglas came up with this novel gantry in 1963. Here a load of palletised Bedford parts are unloaded from a semi trailer drawn by a Tugmaster.

Tugmasters come in all shapes and sizes. This is a recent P111 with 176 bhp Perkins V8. It has 4x4, three power shift gears forward and reverse with torque converter and can handle aircraft of up to 440,000 lbs or, in this case, tanks in a repair shop.

Rather than buy a £¼ million crane, the GPO invested £17,000 in this Tugmaster which handles 70 ton containers of submarine cable with the help of hover pads powered by its inbuilt compressor.

Royce engined gritter/plough chassis for the new M1 motorway with automatic transmission and a top speed of 40 mph at 20 tons gvw. One final fling with forestry tractors was a four wheel drive and four wheel steer design with ground anchor and 25,000 lb Douglas winch, whilst for BOAC, Douglas made a remarkable Cargomaster with chest-high cab and scissor lift body and moving floor for loading aircraft.

Perhaps the most remarkable products of all were a forward control bus chassis for South Africa, fitted at its destination with a Clark and Kent single deck body, some enormous mobile gantries in 1963 that could straddle containers of up to 25ft x 9ft x 10ft 6ins for dockside trans-shipment, and a special lorry for the Swedish armaments firm Bofors in 1962. This last mentioned machine was a bonneted, front wheel drive design which had its chassis members built up the sides of the load space rather than under it. The load platform could be mechanically lowered to the ground and raised to whatever height was required. Unfortunately, when loaded, it turned out to be too heavy for a bridge at the Bofors works so instead it was sold to Bristol-Siddeley, who apparently still use it today. One of the most special recent 'specials' was a compressor truck for the GPO which, for £17,000, did away with the need for a £¼ million crane. It inflated a skirt under 70 ton pallets of submarine cable and enabled them to be pushed around South-ampton docks with ease.

By the time that Leslie Douglas died in the mid-sixties, his firm was wholly involved with tugs for docks and airports. His widow and daughter, Tania, remain directors of the company today and take a close interest in the works. Each tug takes around three weeks to make and there is no production line. Instead, all the fabrications and components are supplied to an assembly bay where each vehicle is built up by a two man team, who are joined occasionally by the resident electrician. Simultaneously, a dozen or more tugs and tractors are built but each stays with its same two

assemblers until ready for test, after which any rectification is in the hands of the original builders. The vehicles are very robustly built (even the bodywork/cab is made of 3/16in mild steel plate) to withstand years of knocks and the very high stresses involved in heavy towing. The dock-side tractors have to be able to handle everything that comes off the ferries, and this includes trailers that with their tractive units gross 42 tonnes on the Continent. The fifth wheel on the Douglas can be hydraulically raised to suit all heights of trailer attachment and most journeys are under a mile and may consist of dozens of separate journeys in tight situations. Power-shift transmission takes a lot of the strain out of the transmission and a wide variety of engines have been used, including Perkins, Bedford, Leyland and Caterpillar. A recent innovation has been the licence assembly of Douglas tugs in Spain.

Though new Douglas trucks may not be seen again, the chances are that wherever you travel by sea or air, you will find some form of Tugmaster at work keeping the name of Douglas in the forefront of specialised vehicles.

Typical of today's Tugmasters in service with around 50 airlines is this 1976 low profile DC 14/4. It weighs 72 tons, has 4x4 and four wheel steering, and is powered by a 380 bhp Deutz air-cooled diesel. Note the low cab at the other end for use when pushing.

Latest in the range of Ro-Ro elevating fifth wheel Tugmasters is this tilt cab NS8 for up to 65 tons gtv. It has the Leyland 690 turbo six cylinder diesel developing 250 bhp and central controls to enable the driver to face in either direction.

# REVIEWS

**THE GOLDEN YEARS OF TRUCKING.** [Ontario Trucking Association, available from Connoisseur Carbooks. £7.05.] This book was published to commemorate 50 years of the Ontario Trucking Association and its price is kept down by lots of advertisements from member haulage companies, many of which show early vehicles. Frankly, a lot of the sections dealing with Canadian legislation and the birth pangs of the OTA are rather dull, but do not be put off, because there is a splendid section, accounting for around a third of the book, on the history of Canadian trucking. It is by our old friend Rolland Jerry, who knows what he is talking about. Obviously, most of his story and photographs concern American vehicles and his treatment of early to mid-thirties sales successes by Commer, Thornycroft, Leyland and Gardner are largely ignored, but one can excuse this to learn about Gotfredson and the other early Canadian manufacturers. I should have liked to see this history brought up to date so that such recent contenders as CCC (whose Canadian factory has just closed, though they continue to make specialised trucks in America), Canadian Kenworth, Hayes, Sicard, Pacific, Rubber Railroad and Scot could be told. However, one really obscure modern truck, the Peninsular, is illustrated and Sicard and Hayes are covered briefly. We will throw the pages of *VINTAGE TRUCK ANNUAL No 2* open to Rolland Jerry to make good these omissions, but otherwise can thoroughly recommend his book.

**HISTORISCH OVERZICHT VAN DE NEDERLANDSE AUTOMOBIEL INDUSTRIE by M Wallast.** [Vitgeverij Omniboek, Postbus 130, Kampen, De Haag, Netherlands. £47.40.] From the title you can see the immediate problem with this book! However, do not be deterred because Dutch is one of those languages that sounds incomprehensible but makes quite a lot of sense when seen in print. The book contains good potted histories of every firm that has made cars, trucks and buses in Holland and has lots of good photographs. Understandably, DAF takes up a sizeable chunk, and Spyker, who did not do much in the commercial line, also accounts for a lot of pages. Nevertheless, all the obscure truck makers are there, including that curious current brigade of army truck converters turned *pukka* manufacturers - Terberg, RAM and Ginaf, as well as FTF (see the *Motor Panels* article) and Spijkstaal, who make mobile shops. Most interesting to this reviewer is AS, who were contemporaries of Gilford in Britain and made a very similar range of vehicles with Lycoming engines. Then there is the equally US-inspired Ten Cate of the thirties and forties fitted with White and Hercules engines. Other firms whose stories are told in detail are Hoek, who made early steam wagons, Hogra with Perkins and Steyr engined trucks in the fifties, Van Twist, who did strange things to Seddons, Kromhout, who were Gardner licencees and made trucks from 1935 to 1958 and Verheul, best known for psv's but who made trucks around 1960. Altogether a most interesting book and worthy of translation.

**THE FODEN STORY by Pat Kennett.** [Patrick Stephens Ltd. £6.95.] A certain amount of criticism has been levelled at this author/publisher's *World Truck Series* of books on the grounds that they are insufficiently detailed. As if to prove that they can do a really detailed job of one manufacturer's history, we now have the far weightier Foden story. Undoubtedly, the low cost of the *World Truck Series* has opened up the widest possible market to it, but when one sees how good the Foden book is one can only lament that the other truck makers did not come in for such thorough treatment.

So what is in *The Foden Story*? It starts way back in Walter Hancock's Infant and Autopsy days and shows how Hancock's son set up with a partner to make agricultural and engineering machinery in Cheshire in 1848. His partner Plant's name was dropped in the eighteen sixties and replaced by that of Edwin Foden, who had started as an apprentice with the firm in 1856. From small beginnings they grew to make massive mine winding and industrial engines (two of which survive at Kidwelly and are to be preserved), traction engines, thrashing boxes and, ultimately, steam wagons, of which over 7000 were produced.

A lot of the early Foden photos are well known and, to avoid too much repetition, Pat Kennett has made excellent use of works drawings to show important steam model types. These, of course, have the advantage of 'X-raying' vehicles and showing us their mechanical layout. He has also reproduced some interesting early hand written notes from Edwin Foden and has used a number of useful graphs and tables. Unfortunately, these do not extend to model types, or production runs by year, and there are no figures to show internal combustion engined truck production. Interesting chapters parallel the faltering diesel steps at Foden after E R Foden had gone into retirement and his successful reappearance as an assembled truck maker. In some ways the Seth-Smith account of this in his otherwise disappointing book *The Long Haul* is more detailed, but Pat Kennett has got all the interesting facts condensed into a far more readable form and, incidentally, has managed to fix the greenhouse where the ERF was conceived as ER's daughter's, and not as usually published. The early transition to diesel period is ingeniously covered by reference to company reports of the time, which reveal a disastrous head-in-sand attitude to steam's shortcomings by the apparently incompetent Board during the Depression. (ERF was the only Foden left on the Board and he was constantly overruled - hence his premature retirement.)

We all know how ER's brother, Willy, returned from the life of gentleman farmer in Australia in the early thirties to salvage Fodens Ltd, and this is well told by the author, along with an account of the arrival of the firm's saviour, the DG range.

Entirely new to this reviewer was Foden's involvement with dumptrucks as early as 1937, though we cannot agree with the author's summing up of the diesel situation in 1931 - AEC was earlier than any of the firms in Britain actually mentioned and all, except Albion, were offering proprietary engines or their own engines by the date given. Whilst on the subject of minor moans, the car that E R Foden is shown in is not a Crossley but a Vauxhall, and later on Foden is not given the credit it deserves for having made Britain's first tilt cab truck in 1960.

Amongst the many interesting post-war facts to emerge from the book are the attempted Seddon takeover by both ERF and Foden, Rolls-Royce's attempts to woo Foden, and the revelation that Foden's new factory is closely modelled on Scania's. Truck books in Britain still have some way to go to equal the superb standards of John Montville's *Mack* and James Wagner's *Ford Trucks Since 1905*, but Pat Kennett's *The Foden Story* is a sizeable step in this direction, which could have been attained by the use of far more illustrations with extra detailed captions and more minutiae in the text and tables. On the other hand, this would, no doubt, have doubled the price, so one cannot have it both ways and as it stands it is perhaps the best truck book written so far in Britain.

**TRUCKS: AN ILLUSTRATED HISTORY 1896-1920 by G N Georgano and Carlo Demand.** [Macdonald and Jane's. £14.95.] This is, perhaps, the first truly international book on early trucks, having originally appeared in 1978 in Switzerland (which explains why Saurer figures so prominently in it. Admittedly, this is justified, as their designs were widely produced around the world). The book is lavishly produced (hence the price) with lots of colour drawings by Carlo Demand rubbing shoulders with period black and white photographs. Unfortunately, a lot of these are over-familiar because they depict landmark vehicles - like the no 1 Thornycroft with Sir John T and Gottlieb Daimler with his five tonner. The products of approximately 20 factories are looked at in detail, following an international resumé of truck events, and of these 20, roughly a quarter are British, a quarter American and the rest German, Swiss, Italian and French. It is plainly impossible to do full justice to twenty-four important years in this way and though Nick Georgano is to be congratulated for packing in as much information as he conceivably could, the end result is not entirely satisfactory. For my money, I would have preferred to do without the one dimensional colour drawings and have more text, more makers covered and more period photographs. As it is, we have perhaps the first 'coffee table' truck book, but with, for a pleasant change, an authoritative text.

First edition copyright Marshall, Harris & Baldwin 1979.

ISBN 0 906116 07 4

Published by: Published by: Marshall Harris & Baldwin Ltd.
17 Air Street
London, W.1.

Registered in London 1410311.

Designed by: Brian Harris

Printed by: Plaistow Press Ltd., New Plaistow Road, London, E.15.